THE DICTIONARY OF ESSENTIAL QUOTATIONS

THE DICTIONARY OF ESSENTIAL QUOTATIONS

KEVIN GOLDSTEIN-JACKSON

A HELIX BOOK

ROWMAN & ALLANHELD
Totowa, New Jersey

© 1983 Kevin Goldstein-Jackson

First published in the USA 1983 by Barnes & Noble Books
81 Adams Drive, Totowa, New Jersey 07512

Library of Congress Cataloging in Publication Data
Main entry under title:
The Dictionary of essential quotations.

1 1. Quotations, English. I. Goldstein-Jackson,
Kevin, 1946-
PN6081.D527   1983   828'.02   83-2815
ISBN 0-389-20393-9

Reprinted in 1984 as A HELIX BOOK, published by
Rowman & Allanheld, Publishers (a division of
Littlefield, Adams & Company) 81 Adams Drive,
Totowa, New Jersey, 07512

INTRODUCTION

'All of us forget more than we remember, and therefore it hath been my constant Custom to note down and record whatever I thought of my self, or receiv'd from Men, or Books worth preserving.' These words formed part of Thomas Fuller's collection of 6,496 quotations, *Gnomologia*, published in 1732.

Like Thomas Fuller, for many years it has been my habit to jot down witty and otherwise useful quotations, particularly when I was at university studying philosophy, sociology, politics and law. Then, when I first commenced work on this book in 1978, I added to this by researching many, many, works by the famous and the not-so-well-known, aided by the numerous suggestions of friends and colleagues.

This collection is primarily designed for browsing and as a source book of use to speakers and others who want to find, quickly and easily, a suitable brief quotation to either support their particular argument or to provide some light relief! I also hope it will draw attention to works which are well worth reading in full for their literary merit, philosophy, or humour.

The quotations are listed under subjects — although in many cases it would have been possible to have put the same quotation under two or even ten different subject headings. In the interests of keeping the book of manageable size (and price), the quotations only appear under one heading each. An index of authors is given at the end of the book.

Wherever possible, I have gone to the original source of the quotation to check its accuracy and have retained the original spelling and punctuation of the English quotations where it does not lead to the sense being confused or lost. I have also included a few quotations from Samuel Johnson's *Dictionary* of words which have almost been 'lost' (like *amatorculist* and *cark*) but which seem worth re-introducing into ordinary everyday language.

For quotations from speeches I have endeavoured to discover exactly when and where the speech was made. The one quotation from

Introduction

a speech where the *exact* details are not given is by Nancy Reagan (on women) and this is because Mrs Reagan herself is unable to recall exactly when she first said it! But her kindness in responding to my request has been much appreciated — as has that of many other people quoted in this book.

I am indebted, in particular, to Walter H. Salomon (and his most helpful secretary, Miss Maeve Byrne) for permission to quote from some of his excellent speeches and articles; to R.G. Causton, General Director of Nichiren Shoshu of the United Kingdom for permission to quote from the translations of the work of Nichiren Daishonin; to the Society of Authors on behalf of the Bernard Shaw Estate for permission to quote from the works of George Bernard Shaw; and to Routledge & Kegan Paul Ltd for permission to quote from Father Leslie Walker's translation (by far the best) of *The Discourses of Niccolo Machiavelli*. The staff of South Audley Street and Paddington libraries in London have handled all my requests with patience, perseverance and speed and have produced original versions of many of the works quoted — including *Lacon: or Many Things in a Few Words; Addressed to Those Who Think* by the Rev. C.C. Colton (published in 1821 by Longman, Hurst, Rees, Orme & Brown): *Political Aphorisms, Moral and Philosophical Thoughts of the Emperor Napoleon* collected by Cte. Ate. G. De Liancourt (published in 1848 by T.C. Newby); and Thomas Fuller's *Gnomologia: Adagies and Proverbs; Wise Sentences and Witty Sayings, Ancient and Modern, Foreign and British* (published in 1732 by B. Barker).

As mentioned earlier, many friends and colleagues have assisted me in this work — far too many to mention individually — but I should add that Rachel Davies and my wife, Jenny Mei Leng, provided considerable research assistance, despite the diversions of my daughter Jenkev.

ABROAD

Abroad is unutterably bloody and foreigners are fiends.
— Nancy Mitford (1904-73)
  The Pursuit of Love

ABSENCE

Absence is to love what wind is to fire; it extinguishes the small, it inflames the great.
— Comte de Bussy-Rabutin
  (1618-93)
  Histoire Amoureuse des Gaules

ABSENTEE

Absentee, n. A person with an income who has had the forethought to remove himself from the sphere of exaction.
— Ambrose Bierce (1842-1914?)
  The Devil's Dictionary

ABUSE

Iron, when heated in the flames and pounded, becomes a fine sword. Wise men and saints are tested by abuse.
— Nichiren Daishonin (1222-82)
  The Major Writings of Nichiren Daishonin: Letter from Sado

ACADEMICS

Academic and aristocratic people live in such an uncommon atmosphere that common sense can rarely reach them.
— Samuel Butler (1835-1902)
  Note Books

ACCIDENTS

Accidents will occur in the best-regulated families.
— Charles Dickens (1812-70)
  David Copperfield

ACCOUNTABILITY

Accountability, n. The mother of caution.
— Ambrose Bierce (1842-1914?)
  The Devil's Dictionary

. . . the individual is not accountable to society for his actions, in so far as these concern the interests of no person but himself.
— John Stuart Mill (1806-73)
  On Liberty

ACCUSTOMED

There are no conditions to which a man cannot become accustomed, especially if he sees that all those around him live in the same way.
— Leo Tolstoy (1828-1910)
Anna Karenina

ACHIEVEMENT

Those who believe that they are exclusively in the right are generally those who achieve something.
— Aldous Huxley (1894-1963)
Proper Studies

To achieve great things we must live as though we were never going to die.
— Luc de Clapiers, Marquis de Vauvenargues (1715-47)
Réflexions et Maximes

ACQUAINTANCES

Acquaintance, n. A person whom we know well enough to borrow from, but not well enough to lend to.
— Ambrose Bierce (1842-1914?)
The Devil's Dictionary

We need two kinds of acquaintances, one to complain to, while we boast to the others.
— Logan Pearsall Smith (1865-1946)
Afterthoughts

ACTIONS

The great end of life is not knowledge but action.
— Thomas Henry Huxley (1825-95)
Technical Education

Nothing is ever done in this world until men are prepared to kill one another if it is not done.
— George Bernard Shaw (1856-1950)
Major Barbara, Act III

ADAPTATION

. . . it behoves one to adapt Oneself to the Times if one wants to enjoy Continued Good Fortune.
— Niccolo Machiavelli (1469-1527)
Discourses

ADMINISTRATION

Bad administration, to be sure, can destroy good policy; but good administration can never save bad policy.
— Adlai Stevenson (1900-65)
Speech, Los Angeles,
11 September 1952

ADVANCE

All that is human must retrograde if it does not advance.
— Edward Gibbon (1737-94)
Decline and Fall of the Roman Empire

ADVANTAGES

The wise Man draws more Advantages from his Enemies, than a Fool from his Friends.
— Thomas Fuller (1654-1734)
Gnomologia

ADVERSITY

No man can smile in the face of adversity and mean it.
— Edgar Watson Howe (1853-1937)
Country Town Sayings

ADVERTISING

Doing business without advertising is like winking at a girl in the dark. You know what you are doing, but nobody else does.
— Steuart Henderson Britt (1907-)
New York Herald Tribune,
30 October 1956

You can tell the ideals of a nation by its advertisements.
— Norman Douglas (1868-1952)
South Wind

ADVICE

A woman seldom asks advice until she has bought her wedding ring.
— Joseph Addison (1672-1719)
The Spectator, 4 September 1712

To ask advice is in nine cases out of ten to tout for flattery.
— John Churton Collins
(1848-1908)
Maxims and Reflections

Ill Customs and bad Advice are seldom forgotten.
— Benjamin Franklin (1706-90)
Poor Richard's Almanack, 1742

Everyone thinks himself able to advise another.
— Thomas Fuller (1654-1734)
Gnomologia

Many receive advice, few profit by it.
— Publilius Syrus
(*c*. 1st century, BC)
Maxims

Hasty advice is unreliable.
— Sophocles (*c*. 495-406 BC)
Oedipus Tyrannus

AGE

A man is as old as he's feeling,
A woman as old as she looks.
— Mortimer Collins (1827-76)
The Unknown Quantity

At 20 years of age the Will reigns; at 30 the Wit; at 40 the Judgment.
— Benjamin Franklin (1706-90)
Poor Richard's Almanack, 1741

All would live long, but none would be old.
— Benjamin Franklin
Ibid., 1749

At twenty man is a peacock, at thirty a lion, at forty a camel, at fifty a serpent, at sixty a dog, at seventy an ape, at eighty nothing at all.
— Baltasar Gracián (1601-58)
The Art of Worldly Wisdom

Whenever a man's friends begin to compliment him about looking young, he may be sure that they think he is growing old.
— Washington Irving (1783-1859)
Bracebridge Hall

The four stages of man are infancy, childhood, adolescence and obsolescence.

5

Age / Ambition

- Art Linkletter (1912-)
  *A Child's Garden of
  Misinformation*

Every man desires to live long, but
no man would be old.
- Jonathan Swift (1667-1745)
  Thoughts on Various Subjects

AGREEABLE PERSON

'My idea of an agreeable person,'
said Hugo Bohun, 'is a person
who agrees with me.'
- Benjamin Disraeli (1804-81)
  Lothair

AIMS

There are two things to aim at in life:
first, to get what you want; and after
that, to enjoy it. Only the wisest
of mankind achieve the second.
- Logan Pearsall Smith (1865-1946)
  Afterthoughts

ALLIANCE

Alliance, n. In international politics,
the union of two thieves who have
their hands so deeply inserted in each
other's pocket that they cannot
separately plunder a third.
- Ambrose Bierce (1842-1914?)
  The Devil's Dictionary

It is not a Wise Course to make an
Alliance with a Ruler whose
Reputation is greater than his
Strength.
- Niccolo Machiavelli (1469-1527)
  Discourses

AMATORCULIST

amatorculist. A little insignificant
lover; a pretender to affection.
- Samuel Johnson (1709-84)
  Dictionary

AMBASSADORS

An ambassador is an honest man sent
to lie abroad for the good of his
country.
- Sir Henry Wotton (1568-1639)
  Written in the Album of
  Christopher Fleckmore

AMBITION

The ambitious climbs up high and
perilous stairs, and never cares how
to come down; the desire of rising
hath swallowed up his fear of a fall.
- Thomas Adams (1612-53)
  Diseases of the Soul

Ambition, n. An overmastering desire
to be vilified by enemies while living
and made ridiculous by friends when
dead.
- Ambrose Bierce (1842-1914?)
  The Devil's Dictionary

All ambitions are lawful except those
which climb upward on the miseries
or credulities of mankind.
- Joseph Conrad (1857-1924)
  A Personal Record

'Tis a laudable Ambition, that aims at
being better than his Neighbours.
- Benjamin Franklin (1706-90)
  Poor Richard's Almanack, 1749

In Man, Ambition is the common'st
thing;
Each one, by nature, loves to be
a King.
— Robert Herrick (1591-1674)
Hesperides: Ambition

Men pass from one Ambition to
Another, and, having first striven
against Ill-treatment, inflict it next
upon Others.
— Niccolo Machiavelli (1469-1527)
Discourses

Ambition if it feeds at all, does so on
the ambition of others.
— Susan Sontag (1933-   )
The Benefactor

AMERICA

The United States of America — the
greatest potential force, material,
moral, and spiritual, in the world.
— Goldsworthy Lowes Dickinson
(1862-1932)
The Choice Before Us

The great and admirable strength of
America consists in this, that
America is truly the American people.
— Jacques Maritain (1882-1973)
Reflections on America

America is the greatest of
opportunities and the worst of
influences.
— George Santayana (1863-1952)
The Last Puritan

In the United States there is more
space where nobody is than where
anybody is. That is what makes
America what it is.
— Gertrude Stein (1874-1946)

*The Geographical History of
America*

America is a land of wonders, in
which everything is in constant
motion and every change seems an
improvement.
— Alexis de Tocqueville (1805-59)
Democracy in America

America is God's Crucible, the great
Melting Pot where all the races of
Europe are melting and re-forming!
— Israel Zangwill (1864-1926)
The Melting Pot, Act I

AMERICANS

It cannot be in the interest of Russia
to go on irritating the United States.
There are no people in the world who
are so slow to develop hostile feelings
against a foreign country as the
Americans, and there are no people
who, once estranged, are more
difficult to win back.
— Sir Winston Churchill
(1874-1965)
Speech, House of Commons
5 June 1946

The Americans have little faith. They
rely on the power of the dollar.
— Ralph Waldo Emerson (1803-82)
*Nature, Addresses and Lectures:
Man the Reformer*

We Americans worship the almighty
dollar! Well, it is a worthier god than
Heredity Privilege.
— Mark Twain (1835-1910)
Notebook

I was born an American; I will live an
American; I shall die an American.

— Daniel Webster (1782-1852)
Speech, Senate
17 July 1850

ANARCHY

Anarchy stands for the liberation of
the human mind from the dominion
of religion; the liberation of the
human body from the dominion of
property; liberation from the
shackles and restraints of government.
— Emma Goldman (1869-1940)
Anarchism

ANCESTRY

I can trace my ancestry back to a
protoplasmal primordial atomic
globule.
— W.S. Gilbert (1836-1911)
The Mikado

ANECDOTAGE

When a man fell into his anecdotage
it was a sign for him to retire from
the world.
— Benjamin Disraeli (1804-81)
Lothair

ANGER

A man that does not know how to be
angry does not know how to be good.
— Henry Ward Beecher (1813-87)
Proverbs from Plymouth Pulpit

He that is slow to anger *is* better than
the mighty . . .
— *Bible*, Authorized Version
Proverbs, Ch. 16, v. 32

Whate'er's begun in anger ends in
shame.
— Benjamin Franklin (1706-90)
Poor Richard's Almanack, 1734

Anger is the Fever and Frenzy of
the Soul.
— Thomas Fuller (1654-1734)
Gnomologia

Anger is short-liv'd in a good Man.
— Thomas Fuller
ibid.

Anger is a short madness.
— Horace (65-8 BC)
Epistles

ANGLERS

An Angler eats more than he gets.
— Thomas Fuller (1654-1734)
Gnomologia

ANGLING

Angling: incessant expectation, and
perpetual disappointment.
— Arthur Young (1741-1820)
Travels in France

ANIMALS

An animal that refuses to let another
eat it has the courage of its
convictions, and if it gets eaten dies a
martyr to them.
— Samuel Butler (1835-1902)
Note Books

Animals are such agreeable friends —
they ask no questions, they pass no
criticisms.

– George Eliot (1819-80)
  *Scenes of Clerical Life: Mr Gilfil's
  Love Story*

APPEASER

An appeaser is one who feeds a
crocodile – hoping it will eat him last.
– Sir Winston Churchill
  (1874-1965)
  Reader's Digest, December, 1954

APPLAUSE

Applause is the spur of noble minds,
the end and aim of weak ones.
– Reverend C.C. Colton,
  (1780?-1832)
  Lacon

The applause of a single human being
is of great consequence.
– Samuel Johnson (1709-1784)
  Boswell's Life of Johnson

ARCHITECTS

No person who is not a great sculptor
or painter can be an architect. If he is
not a sculptor or painter, he can only
be a *builder*.
– John Ruskin (1819-1900)
  *Lectures on Architecture and
  Painting*

The physician can bury his mistakes,
but the architect can only advise his
client to plant vines.
– Frank Lloyd Wright (1869-1959)
  New York Times Magazine,
  4 October 1953

ARCHITECTURE

Architecture in general is frozen
music.
– Friedrich von Schelling
  (1775-1854)
  Philosophie der Kunst

ARGUMENTS

Arguments out of a pretty mouth
are unanswerable.
– Joseph Addison (1672-1719)
  Women and Liberty

Never maintain an argument with
heat and clamour, though you think
or know yourself to be in the right;
but give your opinions modestly and
coolly, which is the only way to
convince . . .
– Earl of Chesterfield (1694-1773)
  Letter to his son,
  16 October 1747

The best way I know of to win an
argument is to start by being right.
– Lord Hailsham (1907-   )
  The New York Times,
  16 October 1960

ARMIES

To win a Battle it is essential to
inspire the Army with Confidence
both in Itself and in its General.
– Niccolo Machiavelli (1469-1527)
  Discourses

The army must become one with the
people so that they see it as their
own army. Such an army will be
invincible.

- Mao Tse-tung (1893-1976)
  On Protracted War, May, 1938

An army without culture is a dull-witted army, and a dull-witted army cannot defeat the enemy.
- Mao Tse-tung (1893-1976)
  The United Front in Cultural Work, 30 October 1944

In the army the task of supporting the government and cherishing the people should be handled through the ideological education of every commander and fighter, so that they all thoroughly understand its importance. As long as the army on its part does this job well, the local government and the people will also improve their relations with the army.
- Mao Tse-tung (1893-1976)
  Policy for Work in the Liberated Areas for 1946,
  15 December 1945

ARROGANCE

Guard against arrogance. For anyone in a leading position, this is a matter of principle and an important condition for maintaining unity. Even those who have made no serious mistakes and have achieved very great success in their work should not be arrogant.
- Mao Tse-tung (1893-1976)
  Methods of Work of Party Committees, 13 March 1949

ART

Art is long, time is short.
- Charles Baudelaire

(1821-67)
Le Guignon

The history of art is the history of revivals.
- Samuel Butler (1835-1902)
  Note Books

All that is not pertinent in art is impertinent.
- Samuel Butler
  Ibid.

Art is a jealous mistress, and if a man have a genius for painting, poetry, music, architecture, or philosophy, he makes a bad husband and an ill provider.
- Ralph Waldo Emerson (1803-82)
  Conduct of Life: Wealth

An art is only great and significant if it is one that all may enjoy. The art of a clique is but a plaything.
- Somerset Maugham (1874-1965)
  The Summing Up

Art must be parochial in the beginning to become cosmopolitan in the end.
- George Moore (1852-1933)
  Hail and Farewell

All art constantly aspires towards the condition of music.
- Walter Pater (1839-94)
  The Renaissance

Great art is precisely that which never was, nor will be taught, it is pre-eminently and finally the expression of the spirits of great men.
- John Ruskin (1819-1900)
  Modern Painters

Fine art is that in which the hand, the head, and the heart of man go together.
— John Ruskin (1819-1900)
  The Two Paths

All art is but imitation of nature.
— Seneca (*c.* 4 BC-65 AD)
  Epistles

All art is quite useless.
— Oscar Wilde (1854-1900)
  The Picture of Dorian Gray

To reveal art and conceal the artist is art's aim.
— Oscar Wilde
  Ibid.

Diversity of opinion about a work of art shows that the work is new, complex, and vital.
— Oscar Wilde
  Ibid.

ARTISTS

Artists must be sacrificed to their art. Like bees, they must put their lives into the sting they give.
— Ralph Waldo Emerson (1803-82)
  Letters and Social Aims:
  Inspiration

In other countries, art and literature are left to a lot of shabby bums living in attics and feeding on booze and spaghetti, but in America the successful writer or picture-painter is indistinguishable from any other decent business man.
— Sinclair Lewis (1885-1951)
  Babbitt

The true artist will let his wife starve, his children go barefoot, his mother drudge for his living at seventy, sooner than work at anything but his art.
— George Bernard Shaw
  (1856-1950)
  Man and Superman, Act I

ASPIRATIONS

The young have aspirations that never come to pass, the old have reminiscences of what never happened.
— Saki (H.H. Munro) (1870-1916)
  Reginald at the Carlton

ASSASSINATION

Assassination is the extreme form of censorship.
— George Bernard Shaw
  (1856-1950)
  The Rejected Statement

ATHEISTS

By night an atheist half believes a God.
— Edward Young (1683-1765)
  The Complaint: Night Thoughts

ATTENTION

A man is fit for neither business nor pleasure, who either cannot, or does not, command and direct his attention to the present object, and, in some degree banish, for that time, all other objects from his thoughts.
— Earl of Chesterfield (1694-1773)

11

Letter to his son,
14 April 1747

AUNTS

It is no use telling me that there are
bad aunts and good aunts. At the
core they are all alike. Sooner or
later, out pops the cloven hoof.
— P.G. Wodehouse (1881-1975)
The Code of the Woosters

AUTHORITY

Nothing destroyeth authority so
much as the unequal and untimely
interchange of power pressed too far,
and relaxed too much.
— Francis Bacon (1561-1626)
Essays: Of Empire

AUTHORS

The best authors are always the
severest critics of their own works;
they revise, correct, file, and polish
them, till they think they have
brought them to perfection.
— Earl of Chesterfield (1694-1773)
Letter to his son, 6 May 1751

The praise of ancient authors
proceeds not from the reverence of
the dead, but from the competition
and mutual envy of the living.
— Thomas Hobbes (1588-1679)
Leviathan

What I like in a good author is not
what he says, but what he whispers.
— Logan Pearsall Smith (1865-1946)
Afterthoughts

AUTHORSHIP

There are three difficulties in
authorship; — to write anything
worth the publishing — to find honest
men to publish it — and to get
sensible men to read it.
— Reverend C.C. Colton
(1780?-1832)
Lacon

AVARICE

Avarice, the spur of industry, is so
obstinate a passion, and works its
way through so many real dangers
and difficulties, that it is not likely to
be scared by an imaginary danger,
which is so small that it scarcely
admits of calculation.
— David Hume (1711-76)
Essays: Of Civil Liberty

AVERAGE MAN

The general average of mankind are
not only moderate in intellect, but
also moderate in inclinations: they
have no tastes or wishes strong
enough to incline them to do
anything unusual, and they
consequently do not understand
those who have, and class all such
with the wild and intemperate whom
they are accustomed to look down
upon.
— John Stuart Mill (1806-73)
On Liberty

BABIES

A baby is an inestimable blessing
and bother.

— Mark Twain (1835-1910)
Letter to Annie Webster,
1 September 1876

BACHELORS

Bachelors know more about women
than married men. If they didn't
they'd be married, too.
— H.L. Mencken (1880-1956)
Chrestomathy

BACKFRIEND

backfriend. A friend backwards; that
is, an enemy in secret.
— Samuel Johnson (1709-84)
Dictionary

BAD BREATH

You say you'l kiss me, and I thank
you for it:
But stinking breath, I do as hell
abhorre it.
— Robert Herrick (1591-1674)
*Hesperides: Upon a Free Maid,
with a Foule Breath*

BAD MEN

When bad men combine, the good
must associate; else they will fall, one
by one, an unpitied sacrifice in a
contemptible struggle.
— Edmund Burke (1729-97)
*Thoughts on the Cause of the
Present Discontents*

BAD NEWS

The nature of bad news infects the
teller.
— William Shakespeare (1564-1616)
Antony and Cleopatra, Act I,
Sc. II

BADNESS

No one ever became thoroughly bad
all at once.
— Juvenal (60?-140?)
Satires

BALANCE OF POWER

Those who scoff at 'balance of power
diplomacy' on the world scene
should recognize that the only
alternative to a balance of power is
an imbalance of power — and history
shows us that nothing so drastically
escalates the danger of war as such
an imbalance.
— Richard M. Nixon (1913-   )
Press Conference, 25 June 1972

BALDNESS

. . . what he hath scanted men in hair
he hath given them in wit.
— William Shakespeare (1564-1616)
The Comedy of Errors, Act II,
Sc. II

BALLS

The real business of a ball is either to
look out for a wife, to look after a
wife, or to look after somebody else's
wife.

– R.S. Surtees (1803-64)
Mr Facey Romford's Hounds

BASHFULNESS

Of all our parts, the eyes expresse
The sweetest kind of bashfulnesse.
– Robert Herrick (1591-1674)
Hesperides: Bashfulnesse

BEARDS

I could not endure a husband with a
beard on his face: I had rather lie
in the woollen.
– William Shakespeare (1564-1616)
Much Ado About Nothing,
Act II, Sc. I

BEAUTY

There is no Excellent Beauty that
hath not some strangeness in the
proportion.
– Francis Bacon (1561-1626)
Essays: Of Beauty

If you get simple beauty and
    nought else,
You get about the best thing God
    invents.
– Robert Browning (1812-89)
Fra Lippo Lippi

Everything beautiful has its moment
and then passes away.
– Luis Cernuda (1904-63)
Las Ruinas

Everything has its beauty but not
everyone sees it.
– Confucius (551-479 BC)
Analects

Beauty in things exists in the mind
which contemplates them.
– David Hume (1711-76)
Essays: Of Tragedy

A thing of beauty is a joy for ever.
– John Keats (1795-1821)
Endymion

I'm tired of all this nonsense about
beauty being only skin-deep. That's
deep enough. What do you want – an
adorable pancreas?
– Jean Kerr (1923-   )
The Snake Has All The Lines

Beauty can pierce one like a pain.
– Thomas Mann (1875-1955)
Buddenbrooks

Beauty is but a flower
Which wrinkles will devour . . .
– Thomas Nashe (1567-1601)
In Time Of Pestilence

It is rare to see wisdom allied to
beauty.
– Petronius (*c.* 1st century AD)
Satyricon

Remember that the most beautiful
things in the world are the most
useless; peacocks and lilies for
instance.
– John Ruskin (1819-1900)
The Stones of Venice

I always say beauty is only sin deep.
– Saki (H.H. Munro) (1870-1916)
Reginald: Reginald's Choir Treat

Beauty as we feel it is something
indescribable: what it is or what it
means can never be said.
– George Santayana (1863-1952)
The Sense of Beauty

14

It is amazing how complete is the delusion that beauty is goodness.
- Leo Tolstoy (1828-1910)
  The Kreutzer Sonata

Ask a toad what is beauty . . . he will answer that it is a female with two great round eyes coming out of her little head, a large flat mouth, a yellow belly and a brown back.
- Voltaire (1694-1778)
  Dictionnaire Philosophique

BEHAVIOUR

Behave to your inferiors as you would wish your betters to behave to you.
- Seneca (*c.* 4 BC-65 AD)
  Epistles

BELIEF

If you do not believe in yourself you cannot expect other people to believe in you.
- Cyrus Hepplewaite (1807-1900)
  The Way to Live

BETRAYAL

. . . he who betrays the friend that trusts him, is guilty of a crime, even if his object be to serve another friend to whom he is under greater obligation.
- John Stuart Mill (1806-73)
  Utilitarianism

BIBLE

The Bible may be the truth, but it is not the whole truth and nothing but the truth.
- Samuel Butler (1835-1902)
  Note Books

The Scripture in time of disputes is like an open town in time of war, which serves indifferently the occasions of both parties.
- Alexander Pope (1688-1744)
  Thoughts on Various Subjects

The devil can cite Scripture for his purpose.
- William Shakespeare (1564-1616)
  The Merchant of Venice,
  Act I, Sc. III

BIGOTRY

Bigotry may be roughly defined as the anger of men who have no opinions.
- G.K. Chesterton (1874-1936)
  Heretics

BIOGRAPHY

Read no history: nothing but biography, for that is life without theory.
- Benjamin Disraeli (1804-81)
  Contarini Fleming

BIRTH CONTROL

Women of the working class, especially wage workers, should not have more than two children at most. The average working man can

15

support no more and the average
working woman can take care of no
more in decent fashion.
— Margaret Sanger (1883-1966)
  Family Limitations

BLACK MEN

. . . and the old saying is,
'Black men are pearls in beauteous
ladies' eyes.'
— William Shakespeare (1564-1616)
  The Two Gentlemen of Verona,
  Act V, Sc. II

BLUE

Blue colour is everlastingly appointed
by the Deity to be a source of delight.
— John Ruskin (1819-1900)
  *Lectures on Architecture and
  Painting*

BLUES

Blues are the songs of despair, but
gospel songs are the songs of hope.
— Mahalia Jackson (1911-72)
  Movin' On Up

BLUNDERS

Fools are pleased with their own
Blunders.
— Thomas Fuller (1654-1734)
  Gnomologia

BLUSHING

Man is the only animal that blushes.
Or needs to.

— Mark Twain (1835-1910)
  Following the Equator

BOASTING

He who boasts achieves nothing.
— Lao-tzu (*c*. 604-*c*. 531 BC)
  Tao Te Ching

BOLDNESS

By boldness great fears are concealed.
— Lucan (39-65)
  De Bello Civili

BOOKS

Some books are to be tasted, others
to be swallowed, and some few to be
chewed and digested . . . Some books
also may be read by deputy, and
extracts made of them by others.
— Francis Bacon (1561-1626)
  Essays: Of Studies

The oldest books are still only just
out to those who have not read them.
— Samuel Butler (1835-1902)
  Note Books

'What is the use of a book,' thought
Alice, 'without pictures or
conversations?'
— Lewis Carroll (1832-1898)
  Alice in Wonderland

Most of today's books have an air of
having been written in one day from
books read the night before.
— Nicolas-Sébastien Chamfort
  (1741-94)
  Maximes et pensées

16

The easiest books are generally the best; for, whatever author is obscure and difficult in his own language, certainly does not think clearly.
- Earl of Chesterfield (1694-1773)
  Letter to his son,
  8 February 1750

With books, as with companions, it is of more consequence to know which to avoid, than which to chuse; for good books are as scarce as good companions, and in both instances, all that we can learn from bad ones, is, that so much time has been worse than thrown away.
- Reverend C.C. Colton
  (1780?-1832)
  Lacon

Books are fatal: they are the curse of the human race. Nine-tenths of existing books are nonsense, and the clever books are the refutation of that nonsense. The greatest misfortune that ever befell man was the invention of printing.
- Benjamin Disraeli (1804-81)
  Lothair

Only two classes of books are of universal appeal: the very best and the very worst.
- Ford Madox Ford (1873-1939)
  Joseph Conrad

A Book that is shut, is but a Block.
- Thomas Fuller (1654-1734)
  Gnomologia

I cannot live without books.
- Thomas Jefferson (1743-1826)
  Letter to John Adams,
  10 June 1815

I love to lose myself in other men's minds. When I am not walking, I am reading; I cannot sit and think. Books think for me.
- Charles Lamb (1775-1834)
  Last Essays of Elia: Detached Thoughts on Books and Reading

There can hardly be a stranger commodity in the world than books. Printed by people who don't understand them; sold by people who don't understand them; bound, criticised and read by people who don't understand them, and now even written by people who don't understand them.
- Georg Christoph Lichtenberg
  (1742-99)
  A Doctrine of Scattered Occasions

A book is a mirror: if an ass peers into it, you can't expect an apostle to look out.
- Georg Christoph Lichtenberg
  (1742-99)
  Aphorisms

Books are not absolutely dead things, but do contain a potency of life in them to be as active as that soul was whose progeny they are; nay they do preserve as in a vial the purest efficacy and extraction of that living intellect that bred them.
- John Milton (1608-74)
  Areopagitica

... who kills a man kills a reasonable creature, God's image; but he who destroys a good book, kills reason itself, kills the image of God, as it were in the eye.
- John Milton
  Ibid.

Books / Bores

A good book is the precious life-blood of a master spirit, embalmed and treasured up on purpose to a life beyond life.
— John Milton
  Ibid.

A book that furnishes no quotations is, *me judice*, no book — it is a plaything.
— Thomas Love Peacock
  (1785-1866)
  Crotchet Castle

I hate books, for they only teach people to talk about what they do not understand.
— Jean Jacques Rousseau (1712-78)
  Émile

If a book is worth reading, it is worth buying.
— John Ruskin (1819-1900)
  Sesame and Lilies

All books are divisible into two classes: the books of the hour, and the books of all time.
— John Ruskin
  Ibid.

Books are good enough in their own way, but they are a mighty bloodless substitute for life.
— Robert Louis Stevenson
  (1850-94)
  An Apology for Idlers

Of all the needs a book has the chief need is that it be readable.
— Anthony Trollope (1815-82)
  Autobiography

A good book is the best of friends, the same today and for ever.
— Martin Farquhar Tupper

(1810-89)
Proverbial Philosophy

Much is written of the power of the Press, a power which may last but a day; by comparison, little is heard of the power of books, which may endure for generations.
— Sir Stanley Unwin (1884-1968)
  The Truth About Publishing

There is no such thing as a moral or an immoral book. Books are well written, or badly written. That is all.
— Oscar Wilde (1854-1900)
  The Picture of Dorian Gray

In the old days books were written by men of letters and read by the public. Nowadays books are written by the public and read by nobody.
— Oscar Wilde (1854-1900)
  A Few Maxims for the Instruction of the Over-Educated

BOREDOM

Boredom: the desire for desires.
— Leo Tolstoy (1828-1910)
  Anna Karenina

BORES

Bore, n. A person who talks when you wish him to listen.
— Ambrose Bierce (1842-1914?)
  The Devil's Dictionary

It is the peculiarity of the bore that he is the last person to find himself out.
— Oliver Wendell Holmes (1809-94)
  Over the Teacups

We frequently forgive those who bore
us, but cannot forgive those whom
we bore.
- Duc de La Rochefoucauld
  (1613-80)
  Maxims

A bore is a man who, when you ask
him how he is, tells you.
- Bert Leston Taylor (1866-1921)
  The So-Called Human Race

All kinds of people are good except
those that are boring.
- Voltaire (1694-1778)
  L'Enfant Prodigue

BORROWERS

. . . the borrower *is* servant to the
lender.
- *Bible*, Authorized version
  Proverbs, Ch. 22, v. 7

BORROWING

Let us all be happy and live within
our means, even if we have to borrow
the money to do it with.
- Artemus Ward (Charles Farrar
  Browne) (1834-67)
  Science and Natural History

Neither a borrower nor a lender be;
For loan oft loses both itself
  and friend,
And borrowing dulls the edge of
  husbandry.
- William Shakespeare (1564-1616)
  Hamlet, Act I, Sc. III

BOTTOM

I have found some of the best reasons
I ever had for remaining at the
bottom simply by looking at the men
at the top.
- Frank Colby (1865-1925)
  Essays

BOUNDARIES

No man has a right to fix the
boundary of the march of a nation;
no man has a right to say to his
country – thus far shalt thou go and
no further.
- Charles Stewart Parnell (1846-91)
  Speech at Cork, Eire,
  21 January 1885

BOURGEOIS

Bourgeois is the epithet which the
riff-raff apply to what is respectable
and the aristocracy to what is decent.
- Anthony Hope (1863-1933)
  The Dolly Dialogues

BRAVERY

Any coward can fight a battle when
he's sure of winning; but give me the
man who has pluck to fight when
he's sure of losing.
- George Eliot (1819-80)
  Janet's Repentance

Some have been thought brave,
because they were afraid to run away.
- Thomas Fuller (1654-1734)
  Gnomologia

Bravery / Bureaucracy

Any fool can be brave on a battle
field when it's be brave or else
be killed.
- Margaret Mitchell (1900-49)
  Gone with the Wind

Bravery never goes out of fashion.
- William Makepeace Thackeray
  (1811-63)
  The Four Georges: George II

BRAWLING WOMEN

It is better to dwell in a corner of
the housetop, than with a brawling
woman in a wide house.
- *Bible*, Authorized version
  Proverbs, Ch. 21, v. 9

BREEDING

Men are generally more careful of the
breed of their horses and dogs than
of their children.
- William Penn (1644-1718)
  *Some Fruits of Solitude, in
  Reflections and Maxims relating
  to the Conduct of Human Life*

BRITISH

The British nation is unique in this
respect. They are the only people
who like to be told how bad things
are, who like to be told the worst.
- Sir Winston Churchill
  (1874-1965)
  Speech, House of Commons,
  10 June 1941

We are overspent, overborrowed,
overgoverned, overtaxed,
overmanned, underpoliced,

underdefended and rather badly
educated.
- Sir Keith Joseph (1918-   )
  Sunday Telegraph
  10 June 1979

BRITISH EMPLOYERS

. . . British employers seem to have
gone soft on the job. They lack the
essential meanness needed to make a
business prosper. They see industry
in terms of workers' benefit, a job-
creation scheme, rather than as a way
of making money. They generously
concede demands they should never
have conceded. We are all so
extraordinarily nice that we are not
fit to employ anybody.
- Auberon Waugh (1939-   )
  Sunday Telegraph
  29 August 1982

BUILDING

When we build, let us think that we
build for ever.
- John Ruskin (1819-1900)
  The Seven Lamps of Architecture

BUREAUCRACY

. . . where everything is done through
the bureaucracy, nothing to which
the bureaucracy is really adverse can
be done at all.
- John Stuart Mill (1806-73)
  On Liberty

BUSINESS

If you can build a business up big
enough, it's respectable.
— Will Rogers (1879-1935)
*The Autobiography of
Will Rogers*

BUT

There is always a 'but' in this
imperfect world.
— Anne Brontë (1820-49)
The Tenant of Wildfell Hall

CAMBRIDGE PEOPLE

For Cambridge people rarely smile,
Being urban, squat, and packed
    with guile.
— Rupert Brooke (1887-1915)
The Old Vicarage: Grantchester

CAPITALISM

The inherent vice of capitalism is
the unequal sharing of blessings. The
inherent vice of socialism is the
unequal sharing of miseries.
— Sir Winston Churchill
   (1874-1965)
   Speech, House of Commons,
   22 October 1945

CAREER WOMEN

A career woman who has survived the
hurdle of marriage and maternity
encounters a new obstacle: the
hostility of men.
— Caroline Bird (1915-   )
   Born Female

CARK

to cark. To be careful; to be
solicitous; to be anxious. It is now
very little used, and always in an ill
sense.
— Samuel Johnson (1709-84)
   Dictionary

CATS

When I play with my cat, who knows
whether she is not amusing herself
with me more than I with her?
— Michel Eyquem de Montaigne
   (1533-92)
   Essays

CAUSE

Those who serve the greater cause
may make the cause serve them.
— T.S. Eliot (1888-1965)
   Murder in the Cathedral

CELEBRITIES

A celebrity is a person who works
hard all his life to become known,
then wears dark glasses to avoid
being recognised.
— Fred Allen (John F. Sullivan)
   (1894-1956)
   Treadmill to Oblivion

CENSURE

No man can justly censure or
condemn another, because indeed no
man truly knows another.
— Sir Thomas Browne (1605-82)
   Religio Medici

CENSORSHIP

If all mankind minus one were of
one opinion, and only one person
were of the contrary opinion,
mankind would be no more justified
in silencing that one person, than he,
if he had the power, would be
justified in silencing mankind.
– John Stuart Mill (1806-73)
   On Liberty

But the peculiar evil of silencing the
expression of an opinion is, that it is
robbing the human race; posterity as
well as the existing generation; those
who dissent from the opinion, still
more than those who hold it. If the
opinion is right, they are deprived of
the opportunity of exchanging error
for truth: if wrong, they lose, what
is almost as great a benefit, the
clearer perception and livelier
impression of the truth, produced by
its collision with error.
– John Stuart Mill
   Ibid.

CERTAINTY

But in this world nothing can be said
to be certain, except death and taxes.
– Benjamin Franklin (1706-90),
   Letter to Jean Baptiste Le Roy,
   13 November 1789

CHANCE

A wise Man turns Chance into good
Fortune.
– Thomas Fuller (1654-1734)
   Gnomologia

CHANGE

The absurd man is the one who
never changes.
– Auguste Barthélemy (1796-1867)
   Ma Justification

It is probably true to say that the
largest scope for change still lies in
men's attitude to women, and in
women's attitude to themselves.
– Vera Brittain (1893-1970)
   Lady into Woman

The oldest habit in the world for
resisting change is to complain that
unless the remedy to the disease can
be universally applied it should not
be applied at all. But you must begin
somewhere.
– Sir Winston Churchill
   (1874-1965)
   Speech, House of Commons,
   15 May 1911

CHARACTER

The ultimate measure of a man is not
where he stands in moments of
comfort and convenience, but where
he stands at times of challenge and
controversy.
– Martin Luther King (1929-68)
   Strength to Love

Character is what you are in the dark.
– Dwight L. Moody (1837-99)
   Sermons

Character is much easier kept than
recovered.
– Thomas Paine (1737-1809)
   The American Crisis

CHARITY

Charity degrades those who receive it and hardens those who dispense it.
— George Sand (1804-76)
Consuelo

Charity creates a multitude of sins.
— Oscar Wilde (1854-1900)
The Soul of Man Under Socialism

CHEATING

Nothing is easier than to cheat an honest man.
— Baltasar Gracián (1601-58)
Oráculo Manual

CHEERFULNESS

A merry heart maketh a cheerful countenance . . .
— *Bible*, Authorized version
Proverbs, Ch. 15, v. 13

CHICAGO

. . . you cannot stop the wicked from going to Chicago by killing them.
— Ambrose Bierce (1842-1914?)
Fantastic Fables

CHILDBIRTH

Childbirth is an occupational hazard of being a wife.
— HRH Princess Anne (1950-   )
comment in *Brian Moore Meets Captain Mark Phillips*, TV documentary, 17 April 1981

CHILDHOOD

The childhood shews the man,
As morning shews the day.
— John Milton (1608-74)
Paradise Regained

CHILDREN

Children sweeten labours, but they make misfortunes more bitter.
— Francis Bacon (1561-1626)
Essays: Of Parents and Children

When children stand quiet, they have done some ill.
— George Herbert (1593-1633)
Jacula Prudentum

It still remains unrecognised, that to bring a child into existence without a fair prospect of being able, not only to provide food for its body, but instruction and training for its mind, is a moral crime, both against the unfortunate offspring and against society; and that if the parent does not fulfil this obligation, the State ought to see it fulfilled, at the charge, as far as possible, of the parent.
— John Stuart Mill (1806-73)
On Liberty

I have been assured by a very knowing *American* of my Acquaintance in *London*; that a young healthy Child, well nursed, is, at a Year old, a most delicious, nourishing, and wholesome Food; whether *Stewed, Roasted, Baked*, or *Boiled*; and, I make no doubt, that it will equally serve in a *Fricasie*, or *Ragoust*.
— Jonathan Swift (1667-1745)
A Modest Proposal for Preventing

23

the Children of Poor People in Ireland, from being a Burden to their Parents or Country; and for making them Beneficial to the Publick

Parents of young children should realise that few people, and maybe no one, will find their children as enchanting as they do.
— Barbara Walters (1931-   )
  How to Talk with Practically Anybody about Practically Anything

CHINESE PEOPLE

Nothing and no one can destroy the Chinese people. They are relentless survivors. They are the oldest civilized people on earth. Their civilization passes through phases but its basic characteristics remain the same. They yield, they bend to the wind, but they never break.
— Pearl S. Buck (1892-1973)
  China, Past and Present

CHRISTIANITY

No nations are more warlike than those which profess Christianity.
— Pierre Bayle (1647-1706)
  Pensées sur la Comète

Christianity supplies a Hell for the people who disagree with you and a Heaven for your friends.
— Elbert Hubbard (1856-1915)
  The Note Book

Christianity is the most materialistic of all great religions.
—Archbishop William Temple

(1881-1944)
Reading in *St. John's Gospel*

CHRISTMAS

Christmas won't be Christmas without any presents.
— Louisa May Alcott (1832-88)
  Little Women

CHURCH

The church must be reminded that it is not the master or the servant of the state, but rather the conscience of the state.
— Martin Luther King (1929-68)
  Strength to Love

CIGARS

. . . a woman is only a woman, but a good Cigar is a Smoke.
— Rudyard Kipling (1865-1936)
  The Betrothed

CIRCUMSTANCES

Man is not the creature of circumstances. Circumstances are the creatures of men.
— Benjamin Disraeli (1804-81)
  Vivian Grey

CITIES

No city should be too large for a man to walk out of in a morning.
— Cyril Connolly (1903-74)
  The Unquiet Grave

CITIZEN

If a man be gracious and courteous to strangers, it shews he is a citizen of the world.
– Francis Bacon (1561-1626)
Essays: Of Goodness, and Goodness of Nature

CITIZENSHIP

The first requisite of a good citizen in this Republic of ours is that he shall be able and willing to pull his weight.
– Theodore Roosevelt (1858-1919)
Speech, New York,
11 November 1902

CIVILIZATION

The civilization of one epoch becomes the manure of the next.
– Cyril Connolly (1903-74)
The Unquiet Grave

The true test of civilization is, not the census, nor the size of cities, nor the crops – no, but the kind of man the country turns out.
– Ralph Waldo Emerson (1803-82)
Society and Solitude

A decent provision for the poor is the true test of civilization.
– Samuel Johnson (1709-84)
Boswell's Life of Johnson

Civilization advances by extending the number of important operations which we can perform without thinking about them.
– Alfred North Whitehead

(1861-1947)
An Introduction to Mathematics

CLAIRVOYANT

Clairvoyant, n. A person, commonly a woman, who has the power of seeing that which is invisible to her patron – namely, that he is a blockhead.
– Ambrose Bierce (1842-1914?)
The Devil's Dictionary

CLARITY

Everything that can be thought at all can be thought clearly. Everything that can be said can be said clearly.
– Ludwig Wittgenstein (1889-1951)
Tractatus Logico-philosophicus

CLEVERNESS

Cleverness is not wisdom.
– Euripides (*c.* 485-406 BC)
The Bacchae

A very clever man will know how to hide his cleverness.
– Duc de La Rochefoucauld (1613-80)
Maxims

CLOTHES

Good Clothes open all Doors.
– Thomas Fuller (1654-1734)
Gnomologia

A sweet disorder in the dresse
Kindles in cloathes a wantonnesse.

- Robert Herrick (1591-1674)
  Hesperides: Delight in Disorder

COFFEE

Why do they always put mud into coffee on board steamers? Why does the tea generally taste of boiled boots?
- William Makepeace Thackeray (1811-63)
  The Kickleburys on the Rhine

COLLEGES

Colleges are places where pebbles are polished and diamonds are dimmed.
- Robert G. Ingersoll (1833-99)
  Prose-Poems and Selections

COLONIES

Colonies do not cease to be colonies because they are independent.
- Benjamin Disraeli (1804-81)
  Speech, House of Commons,
  5 February 1863

COLOUR

The purest and most thoughtful minds are those which love colour the most.
- John Ruskin (1819-1900)
  The Stones of Venice

COMMENDATION

There is nothing more universally commended than a fine day; the reason is, that people can commend it without envy.
- William Shenstone (1714-63)
  On Men and Manners

COMEDIANS

Comedians on the stage are invariably suicidal when they get home.
- Elsa Lanchester (1902-   )
  Charles Laughton and I

COMEDY

Comedy is the clash of character. Eliminate character from comedy and you get farce.
- W.B. Yeats (1865-1939)
  Dramatis Personae

COMFORT

He receives comfort like cold porridge.
- William Shakespeare (1564-1616)
  The Tempest, Act II, Sc. I

COMMAND

If you command wisely, you'll be obey'd cheerfully.
- Thomas Fuller (1654-1734)
  Gnomologia

COMMANDMENTS

The Eleventh Commandment: Thou shalt not be found out.
- George Whyte-Melville (1821-78)
  Holmby House

COMMITTEES

A committee is a cul-de-sac down
which ideas are lured and then
quietly strangled.
– Sir Barnett Cocks (1907-   )
   New Scientist
   8 November 1973

What is a committee? A group of the
unwilling, picked from the unfit, to
do the unnecessary.
– Richard Harkness (1907-   )
   New York Herald Tribune
   15 June 1960

COMMON SENSE

You can't teach common sense.
– Cyrus Hepplewaite (1807-1900)
   The Way to Live

COMMUNISM

I will not pretend that, if I had to
choose between Communism and
Nazi-ism, I would choose
Communism. I hope not to be called
upon to survive in the world under a
government of either of those
dispensations.
– Sir Winston Churchill
   (1874-1965)
   Speech, House of Commons,
   14 April 1937

Communism has sometimes
succeeded as a scavenger, but never as
a leader. It has never come to power
in any country that was not
disrupted by war or internal
corruption or both.
– John F. Kennedy (1917-63)
   Address, North Atlantic Treaty

Organisation headquarters,
Naples, Italy, 3 July 1963

COMMUNISTS

A communist must never be
opinionated or domineering, thinking
that he is good in everything while
others are good in nothing; he must
never shut himself up in his little
room, or brag and boast and lord it
over others.
– Mao Tse-tung (1893-1976)
   Speech, Assembly of
   Representatives of the Shensi-
   Kansu-Ningsia Border Region,
   21 November 1941

Communists must listen attentively
to the views of people outside the
Party and let them have their say. If
what they say is right, we ought to
welcome it, and we should learn from
their strong points; if it is wrong, we
should let them finish what they are
saying and then patiently explain
things to them.
– Mao Tse-tung
   Ibid.

Communists must always go into the
whys and wherefores of anything, use
their own heads and carefully think
over whether or not it corresponds to
reality and is really well founded; on
no account should they follow
blindly and encourage slavishness.
– Mao Tse-tung (1893-1976)
   Rectify the Party's Style of Work,
   1 February 1942

Communists must be ready at all
times to stand up for the truth,
because truth is in the interests of
the people; Communists must be

27

ready at all times to correct their mistakes, because mistakes are against the interests of the people.
— Mao Tse-tung (1893-1976)
  On Coalition Government,
  24 April 1945

COMPARISON

'Tis Comparison, that makes Men happy or miserable.
— Thomas Fuller (1654-1734)
  Gnomologia

COMPLACENCY

We must not become complacent over any success. We should check our complacency and constantly criticize our shortcomings, just as we should wash our faces or sweep the floor every day to remove the dirt and keep them clean.
— Mao Tse-tung (1893-1976)
  Get Organized!
  29 November 1943

COMPLAINING

He, that always complains, is never pitied.
— Thomas Fuller (1654-1734)
  Gnomologia

COMPLEXION

A clear complexion is very simple: Never, never pick a pimple.
— Cyrus Hepplewaite (1807-1900)
  The Way to Live

COMPLIMENTS

A compliment is something like a kiss through a veil.
— Victor Hugo (1802-85)
  Les Misérables

Compliment — a thing often paid by people who pay nothing else.
— Horatio Smith (1779-1849)
  The Tin Trumpet

COMPROMISE

Compromise used to mean that half a loaf was better than no bread. Among modern statesmen it really seems to mean that half a loaf is better than a whole loaf.
— G.K. Chesterton (1874-1936)
  What's Wrong with the World

CONCEIT

Self-conceit may lead to self-destruction.
— Aesop (*c*. 550 BC)
  The Frog and the Ox

I've never any pity for conceited people, because I think they carry their comfort about with them.
— George Eliot (1819-80)
  The Mill on the Floss

Talk about conceit as much as you like, it is to human character what salt is to the ocean; it keeps it sweet, and renders it endurable.
— Oliver Wendell Holmes (1809-94)
  The Autocrat of the Breakfast-Table

I say that conceit is just as natural a thing to human minds as a centre is to a circle.
— Oliver Wendell Holmes
  Ibid.

Conceit may puff a man up, but never prop him up.
— John Ruskin (1819-1900)
  Pre-Raphaelitism

As for conceit, what man will do any good who is not conceited? Nobody holds a good opinion of a man who has a low opinion of himself.
— Anthony Trollope (1815-82)
  Orley Farm

CONCERTS

The harmony of a concert, to which you listen with delight, must have on certain classes of minute animals the effect of terrible thunder; perhaps it kills them.
— Voltaire (1694-1778)
  Dictionnaire Philosophique

CONCESSIONS

The concessions of the weak are the concessions of fear.
— Edmund Burke (1729-97)
  Speech on conciliation with America, 22 March 1775

CONFIDENCE

He who has confidence in himself will lead the rest.
— Horace (65-8 BC)
  Epistles

CONFORMITY

. . . even in what people do for pleasure, conformity is the first thing thought of; they like in crowds; they exercise choice only among things commonly done: peculiarity of taste, eccentricity of conduct, are shunned equally with crimes: until by dint of not following their own nature they have no nature to follow: their human capacities are withered and starved: they become incapable of any strong wishes or native pleasures, and are generally without either opinions or feelings of home growth, or properly their own.
— John Stuart Mill (1806-73)
  On Liberty

Conformity is the jailer of freedom and the enemy of growth.
— John F. Kennedy (1917-63)
  Address, United Nations General Assembly, 25 September 1961

CONQUEST

The right of conquest has no foundation other than the right of the strongest.
— Jean Jacques Rousseau (1712-78)
  Du Contrat Social

CONSCIENCE

A clear Conscience can bear any Trouble.
— Thomas Fuller (1654-1734)
  Gnomologia

A clear Conscience laughs at false accusations.

– Thomas Fuller
  Ibid.

Conscience is the inner voice which
warns us that someone may be
looking.
– H.L. Mencken (1880-1956)
  Chrestomathy

There is no witness so dreadful, no
accuser so terrible as the conscience
that dwells in the heart of every man.
– Polybius (*c*. 208-*c*. 126 BC)
  History

Even when there is no law, there is
conscience.
– Publilius Syrus
  (*c*. 1st century BC)
  Maxims

Conscience has no more to do with
gallantry than it has with politics.
– Richard Brinsley Sheridan
  (1751-1816)
  The Duenna, Act II

Most people sell their souls and live
with a good conscience on the
proceeds.
– Logan Pearsall Smith (1865-1946)
  Afterthoughts

Conscience is God's presence in man.
– Emanuel Swedenborg
  (1688-1772)
  Arcana Coelesta

Conscience and cowardice are really
the same things.
– Oscar Wilde (1854-1900)
  The Picture of Dorian Gray

CONSEQUENCES

Logical consequences are the
scarecrows of fools and the beacons
of wise men.
– Thomas Henry Huxley (1825-95)
  Animal Automatism

CONSERVATIVE
GOVERNMENT

A Conservative government is an
organized hypocrisy.
– Benjamin Disraeli (1804-81)
  Speech, House of Commons,
  17 March 1845 .

CONSERVATIVES

Conservative, n. A statesman who is
enamored of existing evils, as
distinguished from the Liberal, who
wishes to replace them with others.
– Ambrose Bierce (1842-1914?)
  The Devil's Dictionary

A conservative is a man who is too
cowardly to fight and too fat to run.
– Elbert Hubbard (1856-1915)
  Epigrams

A conservative is a man with two
perfectly good legs who, however, has
never learned to walk forwards . . .
– Franklin Delano Roosevelt
  (1882-1945)
  Radio broadcast,
  26 October 1939

CONSPIRACY

People of the same trade seldom
meet together, even for merriment

and diversion, but the conversation ends in a conspiracy against the public, or in some contrivance to raise prices.
— Adam Smith (1723-90)
  The Wealth of Nations

CONSTITUTION

A constitution should be framed so as not to impede the action of government, nor force the government to its violation.
— Napoleon Bonaparte (1769-1821)
  Political Aphorisms, Moral and Philosophical Thoughts of the Emperor Napoleon, collected by Cte. Ate. G. De Liancourt

There exists not in the world one constitution which is followed to the letter.
— Napoleon Bonaparte (1769-1821)
  Ibid.

CONSUL

Consul, n. In American politics, a person who having failed to secure an office from the people is given one by the Administration on condition that he leave the country.
— Ambrose Bierce (1842-1914?)
  The Devil's Dictionary

CONSULT

Consult, v.t. To seek another's approval of a course already decided on.
— Ambrose Bierce (1842-1914?)
  The Devil's Dictionary

CONSULTATION

Well, one can always consult a man and ask him: 'Would you like your head cut off tomorrow?' and after he has said: 'I would rather not', cut it off. Consultation is a vague and elastic term.
— Sir Winston Churchill
  (1874-1965)
  Speech, House of Commons,
  7 May 1947

CONTEMPT

Contempt, n. The feeling of a prudent man for an enemy who is too formidable safely to be opposed.
— Ambrose Bierce (1842-1914?)
  The Devil's Dictionary

There is nothing that people bear more impatiently, or forgive less, than contempt; and an injury is much sooner forgotten than an insult.
— Earl of Chesterfield (1694-1773)
  Letter to his son, 9 October 1746

CONTENTMENT

To be content, look backward on those who possess less than yourself, not forward on those who possess more.
— Benjamin Franklin (1706-90)
  Poor Richard's Almanack, 1757

I only ask that Fortune send
A *little* more than I shall spend.
— Oliver Wendell Holmes (1809-94)
  Contentment

31

CONTRADICTION

The well-bred contradict other people. The wise contradict themselves.
– Oscar Wilde (1854-1900)
  'Phrases and Philosophies for the Use of the Young', *Chameleon*, December, 1894

CONTROVERSY

It is not he who gains the exact point in dispute who scores most in controversy – but he who has shown the better temper.
– Samuel Butler (1835-1902)
  Note Books

CONVERSATION

The characters of Kings and great men are only to be learned in conversation; for they are never fairly written during their lives.
– Earl of Chesterfield (1694-1773)
  Letter to his son, 26 July 1748

Conversation is the music of the mind, an intellectual orchestra where all the instruments should bear a part, but where none should play together.
– Reverend C.C. Colton (1780?-1832)
  Lacon

Blessed is the man who, having nothing to say, abstains from giving wordy evidence of the fact.
– George Eliot (1819-80)
  The Impressions of Theophrastus Such

The Wit of Conversation consists more in finding it in others, than shewing a great deal yourself. He who goes out of your Company pleased with his own Facetiousness and Ingenuity, will the sooner come into it again.
– Benjamin Franklin (1706-90)
  Poor Richard's Almanack, 1756

That is the happiest conversation where there is no competition, no vanity, but a calm quiet interchange of sentiments.
– Samuel Johnson (1709-84)
  Boswell's Life of Johnson

CONVERSATIONALISTS

A gossip is one who talks to you about others; a bore is one who talks to you about himself; a brilliant conversationalist is one who talks to you about yourself.
– Lisa Kirk (1925-)
  New York Journal-American, 9 March 1954

CONVERSION

You have not converted a man because you have silenced him.
– Lord Morley (Viscount Morley of Blackburn) (1838-1923)
  Rousseau

CONVICTION

The one serious conviction that a man should have is that nothing is to be taken too seriously.
– Samuel Butler (1835-1902)
  Note Books

COOKERY

Cookery is become an art, a noble science: cooks are gentlemen.
– Robert Burton (1577-1640)
   Anatomy of Melancholy

CORRUPTION

Corruption is like a ball of snow: whence once set a-rolling it must increase.
– Reverend C.C. Colton
   (1780?-1832)
   Lacon

Corruption, the most infallible symptom of constitutional liberty.
– Edward Gibbon (1737-94)
   The Decline and Fall of the Roman Empire

COUNTRIES

I think that to get under the surface and really appreciate the beauty of any country, one has to go there poor.
– Grace Moore (1901-47)
   You're Only Human Once

COURTSHIP

Better be courted and jilted
Than never be courted at all.
– Thomas Campbell (1777-1844)
   The Jilted Nymph

Courtship to marriage, as a very witty prologue to a very dull Play.
– William Congreve (1670-1729)
   The Old Bachelor

COWARDICE

As an old soldier I admit the cowardice: it's as universal as seasickness, and matters just as little.
– George Bernard Shaw
   (1856-1950)
   Man and Superman, Act III

COWARDS

Many would be Cowards if they had Courage enough.
– Thomas Fuller (1654-1734)
   Gnomologia

CRAVINGS

There is no stronger craving in the world than that of the rich for titles, except that of the titled for riches.
– Hesketh Pearson (1887-1964)
   The Marrying Americans

CREDIT

There can be no other test of the credit of a country than the price at which it can borrow.
– Sir Winston Churchill
   (1874-1965)
   Speech, House of Commons,
   2 June 1908

CREDITORS

Creditors have better memories than debtors.
– Benjamin Franklin (1706-90)
   Poor Richard's Almanack, 1736

CRIME

Urban squalor with its economic,
social and psychological deprivation
is held up as a banner headline to
explain the rise in crime. Let us be
in no doubt that poverty and
deprivation are social injustices which
we should seek to remedy. To use
them to justify crime, however, is to
deny man's freedom of choice and
grossly to insult millions of people
who are poor, deprived and honest.
- Sir David McNee (1925-   )
  Speech, McAlpine Christmas
  luncheon, 7 December 1978

To conceal a crime, another must be
committed.
- Seneca (c. 4 BC-65 AD)
  Hippolytus

CRITICISM

I am bound by my own definition of
criticism: a disinterested endeavour
to learn and propagate the best that
is known and thought in the world.
- Matthew Arnold (1822-88)
  *The Function of Criticism at the
  Present Time*

I do not resent criticism, even when,
for the sake of emphasis, it parts for
the time with reality.
- Sir Winston Churchill
  (1874-1965)
  Speech, House of Commons,
  22 January 1941

Criticism is easy, art is difficult.
- Destouches (Philippe Néricault)
  (1680-1754)
  Le Glorieux, Act II

I have never found, in a long
experience of politics, that criticism
is ever inhibited by ignorance.
- Harold Macmillan (1894-   )
  Wall Street Journal,
  13 August 1963

As for criticism, do it in good time;
don't get into the habit of criticizing
only after the event.
- Mao Tse-tung (1893-1976)
  *On the Question of Agricultural
  Co-operation*, 31 July 1955

People ask you for criticism, but they
only want praise.
- Somerset Maugham (1874-1965)
  Of Human Bondage

CRITICS

Critics generally come to be critics
not by reason of their fitness for this,
but of their unfitness for anything
else. Books should be tried by judge
and jury as though they were a crime,
and counsel should be heard on both
sides.
- Samuel Butler (1835-1902)
  Note Books

A man must serve his time to
  every trade
Save censure – critics all are ready
  made.
- Lord Byron (1788-1824)
  *English Bards and Scotch
  Reviewers*

Reviewers are usually people who
would have been poets, historians,
biographers, if they could: they have
tried their talents at one or the other,
and have failed; therefore they turn
critics.

– Samuel Taylor Coleridge
  (1772-1834)
  Lectures: Shakespeare and Milton

You know who the critics are? The men who have failed in literature and art.
– Benjamin Disraeli (1804-81)
  Lothair

The good critic is he who relates the adventures of his soul among masterpieces.
– Anatole France (1844-1924)
  La Vie Littéraire

The lot of critics is to be remembered by what they failed to understand.
– George Moore (1852-1933)
  Impressions and Opinions

He who criticizes another needs himself to be outstanding.
– Plautus (254-184 BC)
  Truculentus

CRUCIAL

I'm like a table leg around here – crucial, but forever scuffed.
– Jim Hiley (1946-   )
  The Prodigal Father

CRUELTY

Cruelty can only be justified by necessity.
– Napoleon Bonaparte (1769-1821)
  Political Aphorisms, Moral and Philosophical Thoughts of the Emperor Napoleon, collected by Cte. Ate. G. De Liancourt

I must be cruel only to be kind.
– William Shakespeare (1564-1616)
  Hamlet, Act III, Sc. IV

CULTURE

Culture, the acquainting ourselves with the best that has been known and said in the world, and thus with the history of the human spirit.
– Matthew Arnold (1822-88)
  Literature and Dogma

A man should be just cultured enough to be able to look with suspicion upon culture at first, not second hand.
– Samuel Butler (1835-1902)
  Note Books

CUNNING

The weak in courage is strong in cunning.
– William Blake (1757-1827)
  The Marriage of Heaven and Hell: Proverbs of Hell

CURIOSITY

Disinterested intellectual curiosity is the life blood of real civilisation.
– G.M. Trevelyan (1876-1962)
  English Social History

CUSTOMS

Customs represent the experience of mankind.
–   Henry Ward Beecher (1813-87)
  Proverbs from Plymouth Pulpit

Custom is the Guide of the Ignorant.
— Thomas Fuller (1654-1734)
  Gnomologia

Custom without Reason, is but an ancient Error
— Thomas Fuller
  Ibid.

Custom is the Plague of wise Men, and the Idol of Fools
— Thomas Fuller
  Ibid.

Custom, then, is the great guide of human life
— David Hume (1711-76)
  An Enquiry Concerning Human Understanding

He who proposes to change an Old-established Form of Government in an Autonomous State should retain at least the Shadow of its Ancient Customs.
— Niccolo Machiavelli (1469-1527)
  Discourses

CYNICISM

Cynicism is intellectual dandyism.
— George Meredith (1828-1909)
  The Egoist

DANCING

Dancing is in itself a very trifling, silly thing; but it is one of those established follies to which people of sense are sometimes obliged to conform; and then they should be able to do it well.
— Earl of Chesterfield
  (1694-1773)

  Letter to his son,
  19 November 1745

Dancing is the loftiest, the most moving, the most beautiful of the arts, because it is no mere translation or abstraction from life; it is life itself.
— Havelock Ellis (1859-1939)
  The Dance of Life

DANGER

Danger, the spur of all great minds.
— George Chapman (1559?-1634)
  The Revenge of Bussy d'Ambois,
  Act V

Familiarity with danger makes a brave man braver, but less daring.
— Herman Melville (1819-91)
  White Jacket

DATED

Nothing so dates a man as to decry the younger generation.
— Adlai Stevenson (1900-65)
  Speech, University of Wisconsin, Madison, USA, 8 October 1952

DAUGHTERS

An undutiful Daughter, will prove an unmanageable Wife.
— Benjamin Franklin (1706-90)
  Poor Richard's Almanack, 1752

DEATH

To die will be an awfully big adventure.

– J.M. Barrie (1860-1937)
  Peter Pan

Death is only a larger kind of going
abroad.
– Samuel Butler (1835-1902)
  Note Books

No one can escape death once he is
born as a human being, so why do
you not practise in preparation for
the next life?
– Nichiren Daishonin (1222-82)
  *The Major Writings of Nichiren
  Daishonin: Letter to Niike*

The bodies of those that made such
a noise and tumult when alive, when
dead, lie as quietly among the graves
of their neighbours as any others.
– Jonathan Edwards (1629-1712)
  Procrastination

It hath been often said, that it is not
death, but dying which is terrible.
– Henry Fielding (1707-54)
  Amelia

Dying is as natural as living.
– Thomas Fuller (1654-1734)
  Gnomologia

Men fear Death, as Children fear
going in the Dark.
– Thomas Fuller
  Ibid.

We do not die wholly at our deaths:
we have mouldered away gradually
long before. Death only consigns the
last fragments of what we were to
the grave.
– William Hazlitt (1778-1830)
  *On the Feeling of Immortality
  in Youth*

I am always grieved when a man of
real talent dies, for the world needs
such men more than Heaven does.
– Georg Christoph Lichtenberg
  (1742-99)
  Aphorisms

One only dies once, and then it's for
such a long time.
– Molière (1622-73)
  Le Dépit Amoureux

As men, we are all equal in the
presence of death.
– Publilius Syrus
  (*c.* 1st century BC)
  Maxims

Waldo is one of those people who
would be enormously improved by
death.
– Saki (H.H. Munro) (1870-1916)
  *Beasts and Super-Beasts: The
  Feast of Nemesis*

Fear of death is worse than dying.
– Friedrich von Schiller
  (1759-1805)
  Die Räuber

. . . death, as the Psalmist saith, is
certain to all; all shall die.
– William Shakespeare (1564-1616)
  King Henry IV, Pt. II, Act III,
  Sc. II

. . . a man can die but once . . .
– William Shakespeare
  Ibid.

DECENT

Respectable means rich, and decent
means poor. I should die if I heard
my family called decent.

Deception / Democracy

- Thomas Love Peacock
  (1785-1866)
  Crotchet Castle

DECEPTION

It's the easiest Thing in the World for
a Man to deceive himself.
- Benjamin Franklin (1706-90)
  Poor Richard's Almanack, 1746

Nothing is easier than to deceive
one's self.
- Thomas Fuller (1654-1734)
  Gnomologia

The surest method of being deceived
is to believe that one is cleverer than
others.
- Duc de La Rochefoucauld
  (1613-80)
  Maxims

The worst of all deceptions is
self-deception.
- Plato (*c.* 428-348 BC)
  Cratylus

O what a tangled web we weave,
When first we practise to deceive!
- Sir Walter Scott (1771-1832)
  Marmion

DECISIONS

Weak Republics suffer from
Irresolution and cannot reach
Decisions; and, when they do arrive
at one, it is due rather to Necessity
than to Choice.
- Niccolo Machiavelli (1469-1527)
  Discourses

DEFEATS

There are some defeats more
triumphant than victories.
- Michel Eyquem de Montaigne
  (1533-92)
  Essays

DEFECTS

Certain defects are necessary for the
existence of individuality.
- Johann Wolfgang von Goethe
  (1749-1832)
  Elective Affinities

DELAY

Delay is preferable to error.
- Thomas Jefferson (1743-1826)
  Letter to George Washington,
  16 May 1792

DEMOCRACY

Democracy, which means despair of
finding any Heroes to govern you,
and contented putting up with the
want of them.
- Thomas Carlyle (1795-1881)
  Past and Present

The tendency of democracies is, in
all things, to mediocrity.
- James Fenimore Cooper
  (1789-1851)
  The American Democrat

Democracy is only an experiment in
government, and it has the obvious
disadvantage of merely counting
votes instead of weighing them.

— Dean Inge (1860-1954)
  Possible Recovery?

Democracy is a kingless regime infested by many kings who are sometimes more exclusive, tyrannical, and destructive than one, if he be a tyrant.
— Benito Mussolini (1883-1945)
  Fascism

Democracy is clearly most appropriate for countries which enjoy an economic surplus and least appropriate for countries where there is an economic insufficiency.
— David Morris Potter (1910-71)
  People of Plenty: Economic Abundance and the American Character

In the strict sense of the term, a true democracy has never existed, and never will exist.
— Jean Jacques Rousseau (1712-78)
  Du Contrat Social

Our political experiment of democracy, the last refuge of cheap misgovernment.
— George Bernard Shaw
  (1856-1950)
  Man and Superman

Democracy substitutes election by the incompetent many for appointment by the corrupt few.
— George Bernard Shaw
  (1856-1950)
  Man and Superman: Maxims for Revolutionists

The difference between an ordinary democracy and a people's democracy is that in a people's democracy opinion cannot be freely expressed and therefore goes unheeded, whereas in an ordinary democracy like those in the West, opinion can be freely expressed and therefore goes unheeded.
— Peter Ustinov (1921-   )
  Rectorial Address, University of Dundee, 17 October 1968

Democracy means simply the bludgeoning of the people by the people for the people.
— Oscar Wilde (1854-1900)
  The Soul of Man Under Socialism

DENTOPEDALOGY

Dentopedalogy is the science of opening your mouth and putting your foot in it. I've been practising it for years.
— HRH Prince Philip, Duke of Edinburgh (1921-   )
  Speech to UK's General Dental Council, quoted in *Time*, 21 November 1960

DESERT

The desert is an ocean upon which we can walk, it is the image of immensity.
— Napoleon Bonaparte (1769-1821)
  Political Aphorisms, Moral and Philosophical Thoughts of the Emperor Napoleon, collected by Cte. Ate. G. De Liancourt

DESIRE

I think people ought to fulfil sacredly their desires. And this means fulfilling the deepest desire, which is a desire to live unhampered by things

that are extraneous, a desire for pure relationships and living truth.
– D.H. Lawrence (1885-1930)
  Letter to Catherine Carswell,
  16 July 1916

Is it not strange that desire should so many years outlive performance?
– William Shakespeare (1564-1616)
  King Henry IV, Pt. II, Act II,
  Sc. IV

DESPAIR

Despair gives Courage to a Coward.
– Thomas Fuller (1654-1734)
  Gnomologia

He who has never hoped can never despair.
– George Bernard Shaw
  (1856-1950)
  Caesar and Cleopatra, Act IV

DESPOTISM

Despotism is a legitimate mode of government in dealing with barbarians, provided the end be their improvement, and the means justified by actually effecting that end.
– John Stuart Mill (1806-73)
  On Liberty

DESTINY

Destiny leads the willing, but drags the unwilling.
– Thomas Fuller (1654-1734)
  Gnomologia

DETAILS

Men too involved in details usually become unable to deal with great matters.
– Duc de La Rochefoucauld
  (1613-80)
  Maxims

DEVIL

If the devil doesn't exist, but man has created him, he has created him in his own image and likeness.
– Feodor Mikhailovich Dostoevsky
  (1821-81)
  The Brothers Karamazov

A devil
Is a rare juggler, and can cheat
  the eye,
But not corrupt the reason, in
  the throne
Of a pure soul.
– John Ford (*c.* 1586-1639)
  The Lover's Melancholy, Act V

DEXTERITY

Dexterity comes by Experience.
– Thomas Fuller (1654-1734)
  Gnomologia

DIALECT

Dialect words – those terrible marks of the beast to the truly genteel.
– Thomas Hardy (1840-1928)
  The Mayor of Casterbridge

DIARIES

What is a diary as a rule? A document
useful to the person who keeps it,
dull to the contemporary who reads
it, invaluable to the student,
centuries afterwards, who treasures it!
— Ellen Terry (1848-1928)
The Story of My Life

I never travel without my diary. One
should always have something
sensational to read in the train.
— Oscar Wilde (1854-1900)
The Importance of Being Earnest,
Act II

DICTATORS

Dictator, n. The chief of a nation
that prefers the pestilence of
despotism to the plague of anarchy.
— Ambrose Bierce (1842-1914?)
The Devil's Dictionary

One of the disadvantages of
dictatorship is that the dictator is
often dictated to by others — and
what he did to others may often be
done back again to him.
— Sir Winston Churchill
(1874-1965)
Speech, House of Commons,
11 May 1953

DICTATORSHIP

Whenever you have an efficient
government you have a dictatorship.
— Harry S. Truman (1884-1972)
Lecture, Columbia University,
28 April 1959

DIFFICULTIES

Diligence overcomes Difficulties,
Sloth makes them.
— Benjamin Franklin (1706-90)
Poor Richard's Almanack, 1755

DIGNITY

No race can prosper till it learns that
there is as much dignity in tilling a
field as in writing a poem.
— Booker T. Washington
(1856-1915)
Up from Slavery

DIPLOMACY

Diplomacy, n. The patriotic art of
lying for one's country.
— Ambrose Bierce (1842-1914?)
The Devil's Dictionary

The reason for having diplomatic
relations is not to confer a
compliment — but to secure a
convenience.
— Sir Winston Churchill
(1874-1965)
Speech, House of Commons,
17 November 1949

Diplomacy is to do and say
The nastiest thing in the nicest way.
— Isaac Goldberg (1887-1938)
The Reflex

DISAPPOINTMENT

We are born crying, live complaining,
and die disappointed.
— Thomas Fuller (1654-1734)
Gnomologia

DISCIPLINE

Discipline is a symbol of caring to a child.
— Bette Davis (1908-   )
   The Lonely Life

Discipline is the soul of an army.
— George Washington (1732-99)
   Letter of Instructions to the
   Captains of the Virginia
   Regiments, 29 July 1759

DISCONTENTMENT

To complain of the age we live in, to murmer at the present possessors of power, to lament the past, to conceive extravagant hopes of the future, are the common dispositions of the greatest part of mankind.
— Edmund Burke (1729-97)
   *Thoughts on the Cause of the
   Present Discontents*

DISEASE

When a lot of remedies are suggested for a disease, that means it can't be cured.
— Anton Chekhov (1860-1904)
   The Cherry Orchard, Act II

DISLIKE

One who has reached the age of forty and is still disliked will be so until the end.
— Confucius (551-479 BC)
   Analects

DISTRUST

Distrust is the Mother of Safety, but must be kept out of Sight.
— Thomas Fuller (1654-1734)
   Gnomologia

DOCTORS

see under **PHYSICIANS**

DOUBLETHINK

Doublethink means the power of holding two contradictory beliefs in one's mind simultaneously, and accepting both of them.
— George Orwell (1903-50)
   1984

DOUBTS

If a man will begin with certainties, he shall end in doubts; but if he will be content to begin with doubts, he shall end in certainties.
— Francis Bacon (1561-1626)
   Advancement of Learning

He that knows nothing doubts nothing.
— George Herbert (1593-1633)
   Jacula Prudentum

Doubts are more cruel than the worst of truths.
— Molière (1622-73)
   Le Misanthrope, Act III

DRINKING

Life with Fools consists in Drinking;
With the wise Man, Living's Thinking.
— Benjamin Franklin (1706-90)
  Poor Richard's Almanack, 1748

I have very poor and unhappy brains
for drinking: I could well wish
courtesy would invent some other
custom of entertainment.
— William Shakespeare (1564-1616)
  Othello, Act II, Sc. III

DRUMS

The sound of the drum drives out
thought; for that very reason it is the
most military of instruments.
— Joseph Joubert (1754-1824)
  Pensées

DRUNKENNESS

A drunken Night makes a cloudy
Morning.
— Thomas Fuller (1654-1734)
  Gnomologia

Drunkenness turns a Man out of
himself, and leaves a Beast in his
room.
— Thomas Fuller
  Ibid.

Drunkenness is a Pair of Spectacles to
see the Devil and all his works.
— Thomas Fuller
  Ibid.

Drunkenness makes Men Fools; some
Beasts, some Devils.
— Thomas Fuller
  Ibid.

Drunkenness is nothing but voluntary
madness.
— Seneca (4 BC- 65 AD)
  Ad Lucilium

DUTY

Fear God, and keep his
commandments: for this *is* the whole
duty of man.
— *Bible*, Authorized version
  Ecclesiastes, Ch. 12, v. 13

It is seldom very hard to do one's
duty when one knows what it is, but
it is often exceedingly difficult to
find this out.
— Samuel Butler (1835-1902)
  Note Books

What's a man's first duty? The
answer's brief: To be himself.
— Henrik Ibsen (1828-1906)
  Peer Gynt, Act IV

When a stupid man is doing
something he is ashamed of, he
always declares that it is his duty.
— George Bernard Shaw
  (1856-1950)
  Caesar and Cleopatra, Act III

There is no duty we so much
underrate as the duty of being happy.
— Robert Louis Stevenson
  (1850-94)
  Virginibus Puerisque

EATING

Eat to live, and not live to eat.
— Benjamin Franklin (1706-90)
  Poor Richard's Almanack, 1733

Three good meals a day is bad living.
- Benjamin Franklin
  Ibid., 1737

He that never eats too much, will never be lazy.
- Benjamin Franklin
  Ibid., 1756

A full Belly makes a dull Brain . . .
- Benjamin Franklin
  Ibid., 1758

ECCENTRICITY

. . . the amount of eccentricity in a society has generally been proportional to the amount of genius, mental vigour, and moral courage it contained.
- John Stuart Mill (1806-73)
  On Liberty

ECONOMY

Economy is going without something you do want in case you should, some day, want something you probably won't want.
- Anthony Hope (1863-1933)
  The Dolly Dialogues

EDUCATION

Upon the education of the people of this country the fate of this country depends.
- Benjamin Disraeli (1804-81)
  Speech, House of Commons, 15 June 1874

The world exists for the education of each man.

- Ralph Waldo Emerson (1803-82)
  Essays: History

On EDUCATION all our lives depend . . .
- Benjamin Franklin (1706-90)
  Poor Richard's Almanack, 1748

Every man who rises above the common level has received two educations: the first from his teachers; the second, more personal and important, from himself.
- Edward Gibbon (1737-94)
  Memoirs

A general State education is a mere contrivance for moulding people to be exactly like one another . . .
- John Stuart Mill (1806-73)
  On Liberty

Education has for its object the formation of character.
- Herbert Spencer (1820-1903)
  Social Statics

Education is an admirable thing, but it is well to remember from time to time that nothing that is worth knowing can be taught.
- Oscar Wilde (1854-1900)
  'Phrases and Philosophies for the Use of the Young', *Chameleon*, December, 1894

EFFICIENCY

There are only two qualities in the world: efficiency and inefficiency; and only two sorts of people: the efficient and the inefficient.
- George Bernard Shaw (1856-1950)
  John Bull's Other Island, Act IV

EGOTIST

Egotist, n. A person of low taste,
more interested in himself than in me.
— Ambrose Bierce (1842-1914?)
The Devil's Dictionary

ELECTIONS

Elections are won by men and
women chiefly because most people
vote against somebody rather than
for somebody.
— Franklin P. Adams (1881-1960)
Nods and Becks

The ballot is stronger than the bullet.
— Abraham Lincoln (1809-65)
Speech, Bloomington, Illinois,
19 May 1856

Among free men there can be no
successful appeal from the ballot
to the bullet.
— Abraham Lincoln (1809-65),
Letter to James C. Conkling,
26 August 1863

ELECTOR

Elector, n. One who enjoys the
sacred privilege of voting for the man
of another man's choice.
— Ambrose Bierce (1842-1914?)
The Devil's Dictionary

ELOQUENCE

Eloquence depends as much on the
tone, expression and manner of the
speaker as in his choice of words.
— Duc de La Rochefoucauld

(1613-80)
Maxims

True eloquence consists in saying all
that need be said and no more.
— Duc de La Rochefoucauld
Ibid.

EMOTION

Emotion, n. A prostrating disease
caused by a determination of the
heart to the head. It is sometimes
accompanied by a copious discharge
of hydrated chloride of sodium from
the eyes.
— Ambrose Bierce (1842-1914?)
The Devil's Dictionary

EMPIRES

The day of small nations has long
passed away. The day of Empires has
come.
— Joseph Chamberlain (1836-1914)
Speech, Birmingham, England,
12 May 1904

END

This is not the end. It is not even the
beginning of the end. But it is,
perhaps, the end of the beginning.
— Sir Winston Churchill
(1874-1965)
Speech made at the Mansion
House, London,
10 November 1942

ENEMIES

But I say unto you, Love your
enemies, bless them that curse you,
do good to them that hate you, and
pray for them which despitefully
use you, and persecute you.
— *Bible*, Authorized version,
St Matthew, Ch. 5, v. 44

Love your Enemies, for they tell
you your Faults.
— Benjamin Franklin (1706-90)
Poor Richard's Almanack, 1756

A courageous Foe is better than a
cowardly Friend.
— Thomas Fuller (1654-1734)
Gnomologia

So long as governments set the
example of killing their enemies,
private individuals will occasionally
kill theirs.
— Elbert Hubbard (1856-1915)
Contemplations

All our enemies are mortals.
— Paul Valéry (1871-1945)
Mauvaises Pensées

ENERGY

Energy is more attractive than beauty
in a man.
— Louisa May Alcott (1832-88)
Behind a Mask

ENGLAND

Of all the nations in the world the
English are perhaps the least a nation
of pure philosophers.

— Walter Bagehot (1826-77)
The English Constitution

A population sodden with drink,
steeped in vice, eaten up by every
social and physical malady, these are
the denizens of Darkest England
amidst whom my life has been spent.
— William Booth (1829-1912)
*In Darkest England, and the
Way Out*

England is a paradise for women, and
hell for horses: Italy a paradise for
horses, hell for women . . .
— Robert Burton (1577-1640)
Anatomy of Melancholy

England is the paradise of women,
the purgatory of men, and the hell
of horses.
— John Florio (1553?-1625)
Second Frutes

England is a cosy little country,
Excepting for the draughts along
the floor.
— Rudyard Kipling (1865-1936)
The Open Door

The greatness of England is now all
collective; individually small, we only
appear capable of anything great by
our habit of combining; and with
this our moral and religious
philanthropists are perfectly
contented. But it was men of another
stamp than this that made England
what it has been; and men of another
stamp will be needed to prevent its
decline.
— John Stuart Mill (1806-73)
On Liberty

In England we have come to rely
upon a comfortable time lag of fifty

years or a century intervening
between the perception that
something ought to be done and a
serious attempt to do it.
— H.G. Wells (1866-1946)
   *The Work, Wealth and Happiness
   of Mankind*

ENGLISHMEN

One has often wondered whether
upon the whole earth there is
anything so unintelligent, so unapt to
perceive how the world is really
going, as an ordinary young
Englishman of our upper class.
— Matthew Arnold (1822-88)
   Culture and Anarchy

An Englishman thinks he is moral
when he is only uncomfortable.
— George Bernard Shaw
   (1856-1950)
   Man and Superman, Act III

There is nothing so bad or so good
that you will not find Englishmen
doing it; but you will never find an
Englishman in the wrong. He does
everything on principle. He fights
you on patriotic principles; he robs
you on business principles; he
enslaves you on imperial principles;
he supports his king on royal
principles and cuts off his king's
head on republican principles.
— George Bernard Shaw
   (1856-1950)
   The Man of Destiny

How hard it is to make an
Englishman acknowledge that he is
happy.
— William Makepeace Thackeray

(1811-63)
Pendennis

You never find an Englishman among
the underdogs — except in England
of course.
— Evelyn Waugh (1903-66)
   The Loved One

ENJOYMENT

I consider the world as made for me,
not me for the world. It is my maxim
therefore to enjoy it while I can, and
let futurity shift for itself.
— Tobias Smollett (1721-71)
   Roderick Random

ENLIGHTENMENT

Knowing others is wisdom. Knowing
the self is enlightenment.
— Lao-tzu (*c*. 604-*c*. 531 BC)
   Tao Te Ching

ENTERPRISE

It is Enterprise which builds and
improves the world's possessions . . .
If Enterprise is afoot, wealth
accumulates whatever may be
happening to Thrift; and if Enterprise
is asleep, Wealth decays, whatever
Thrift may be doing.
— John Maynard Keynes
   (1883-1946)
   A Treatise on Money

The engine which drives Enterprise is
not Thrift, but Profit.
— John Maynard Keynes
   Ibid.

ENTERPRISES

Beware of all enterprises that require
new clothes.
— Henry David Thoreau (1817-62)
   Walden

ENTHUSIASM

Nothing great was ever achieved
without enthusiasm.
— Ralph Waldo Emerson (1803-82)
   Essays: Circles

ENVELOPE

Envelope, n. The coffin of a
document; the scabbard of a bill; the
husk of a remittance; the bed-gown
of a love-letter.
— Ambrose Bierce (1842-1914?)
   The Devil's Dictionary

ENVY

Nothing sharpens Sight like Envy.
— Thomas Fuller (1654-1734)
   Gnomologia

Envy is better than pity.
— Pindar (*c*. 518-*c*. 438 BC)
   Pythian Odes

EPIGRAM

What is an Epigram? a dwarfish
   whole,
Its body brevity, and wit its soul.
— Samuel Taylor Coleridge
   (1772-1834)
   Epigram

EQUALITY

The men of culture are the true
apostles of equality.
— Matthew Arnold (1822-88)
   Culture and Anarchy

Men are born equal but they are also
born different.
— Erich Fromm (1900-   )
   Escape from Freedom

All of us do not have equal talent,
but all of us should have an equal
opportunity to develop our talents.
— John F. Kennedy (1917-63)
   Address, San Diego State College,
   San Diego, California,
   6 June 1963

That learning belongs not to the
female character, and that the female
mind is not capable of a degree of
improvement equal to that of the
other sex, are narrow and
unphilosophical prejudices.
— Vicesimus Knox (1752-1821)
   Essays

Whatever may be the general
endeavour of a community to render
its members equal and alike, the
personal pride of individuals will
always seek to rise above the line,
and to form somewhere an inequality
to their own advantage.
— Alexis de Tocqueville (1805-59)
   Democracy in America

ERROR

The wisest of the wise may err.
— Aeschylus (525-456 BC)
   Fragments

To err is human, to repent divine,
to persist devilish.
— Benjamin Franklin (1706-90)
  Poor Richard's Almanack, 1742

All men are liable to error; and most
men are, in many points, by passion
or interest, under temptation to it.
— John Locke (1632-1704)
  *Essay on the Human
  Understanding*

Were half the power that fills the
    world with terror,
Were half the wealth bestowed on
    camps and courts,
Given to redeem the human mind
    from error,
There were no need of arsenals
    or forts.
— Henry Wadsworth Longfellow
  (1807-82)
  The Arsenal at Springfield

The fatal tendency of mankind to
leave off thinking about a thing
when no longer doubtful, is the cause
of half their errors.
— John Stuart Mill (1806-73)
  On Liberty

One will rarely err if extreme actions
be ascribed to vanity, ordinary
actions to habit, and mean actions
to fear.
— Friedrich Nietzsche (1844-1900)
  Human, All Too Human

If you shut your door to all errors
truth will be shut out.
— Rabindranath Tagore
  (1861-1941)
  Stray Birds

ESSAY

essay. A loose sally of the mind; an
irregular indigested piece; not a
regular and orderly composition.
— Samuel Johnson (1709-84)
  Dictionary

ETHICS

I can only say that, while my own
opinions as to ethics do not satisfy
me, other people's satisfy me even
less.
— Bertrand Russell (1872-1970)
  Reply to My Critics

EXAMINATIONS

Examinations are formidable even to
the best prepared, for the greatest
fool may ask more than the wisest
man can answer.
— Reverend C.C. Colton
  (1780?-1832)
  Lacon

In examinations the foolish ask
questions that the wise cannot
answer.
— Oscar Wilde (1854-1900)
  'Phrases and Philosophies for the
  Use of the Young', *Chameleon*,
  December, 1894

EXAMPLE

Example is not only the best way of
propagating an opinion, but it is the
only way worth taking into account.
— Samuel Butler (1835-1902)
  Note Books

Example / Experience

A good Example is the best sermon.
— Benjamin Franklin (1706-90)
  Poor Richard's Almanack, 1747

EXCISE

excise. A hateful tax levied upon commodities, and adjudged not by the common judges of property, but wretches hired by those to whom excise is paid.
— Samuel Johnson (1709-84)
  Dictionary

EXCUSES

Any excuse will serve a tyrant.
— Aesop (*c.* 550 BC)
  The Wolf and the Lamb

Bad Excuses are worse than none.
— Thomas Fuller (1654-1734)
  Gnomologia

EXILE

There is no worse fate than to be exiled.
— Euripides (*c.* 485-406 BC)
  Medea

EXPECTATIONS

Blessed is he that expects nothing, for he shall never be disappointed.
— Benjamin Franklin (1706-90)
  Poor Richard's Almanack, 1739

The basic things expected by our people of their political and economic systems are simple. They are: Equality of opportunity for youth and for others. Jobs for those who can work. Security for those who need it. The ending of special privilege for the few. The preservation of civil liberties for all. The enjoyment of the fruits of scientific progress in a wider and constantly rising standard of living. These are the simple, the basic things that must never be lost sight of in the turmoil and unbelievable complexity of our modern world.
— Franklin Delano Roosevelt (1882-1945)
  Speech to Congress,
  6 January 1941

EXPEDIENCY

No man is justified in doing evil on the ground of expediency.
— Theodore Roosevelt (1858-1919)
  The Strenuous Life

EXPERIENCE

All experience is an arch, to build upon.
— Henry Brooks Adams (1838-1918)
  The Education of Henry Adams

Experience teaches slowly, and at the cost of mistakes.
— J.A. Froude (1818-94)
  Short Studies on Great Subjects

At every step the child should be allowed to meet the real experiences of life; the thorns should never be plucked from his roses.
— Ellen Key (1849-1926)
  The Century of the Child

50

Experience is the name everyone
gives to his mistakes.
- Oscar Wilde (1854-1900)
  Lady Windermere's Fan, Act III

EXPERIMENTS OF LIVING

As it is useful that while mankind are
imperfect there should be different
opinions, so it is that there should be
different experiments of living.
- John Stuart Mill (1806-73)
  On Liberty

EXPLANATIONS

I do loathe explanations.
- J.M. Barrie (1860-1937)
  My Lady Nicotine

Never explain. Your friends do not
need it and your enemies will not
believe you anyway.
- Elbert Hubbard (1856-1915)
  The Note Book

EXPORT

I do not believe that a successful
export trade can be founded upon a
starved home market.
- Sir Winston Churchill
  (1874-1965)
  Speech, House of Commons,
  28 October 1947

EXTRAORDINARY CIRCUMSTANCES

To extraordinary circumstances we
must apply extraordinary remedies.
- Napoleon Bonaparte (1769-1821)

*Political Aphorisms, Moral and
Philosophical Thoughts of the
Emperor Napoleon*, collected by
Cte. Ate. G. De Liancourt

FACES

It is the common wonder of all men,
how among so many millions of
faces, there should be none alike.
- Sir Thomas Browne (1605-82)
  Religio Medici

. . . his face is the worst thing about
him . . .
- William Shakespeare (1564-1616)
  Measure for Measure, Act II, Sc. I

FACTS

Facts are stubborn things.
- Ebenezer Elliott (1781-1849)
  Field Husbandry

Facts do not cease to exist because
they are ignored.
- Aldous Huxley (1894-1963)
  A Note on Dogma

Facts speak for themselves.
- Plautus (254-184 BC)
  Aulularia

She always says, my lord, that facts
are like cows. If you look them in the
face hard enough they generally run
away.
- Dorothy L. Sayers (1893-1957)
  Clouds of Witness

Comment is free but facts are sacred.
- C.P. Scott (1846-1932)
  Manchester Guardian,
  6 May 1926

FAILURE

Women can't forgive failure.
- Anton Chekhov (1860-1904)
  The Seagull, Act II

I am afraid that a large part of the object of every country is to throw the blame for an impending failure upon some other country while willing, if possible, to win the Nobel Peace Prize for itself.
- Sir Winston Churchill
  (1874-1965)
  Speech, House of Commons,
  23 November 1932

I would sooner fail than not be among the greatest.
- John Keats (1795-1821)
  Letter to James Hessey,
  9 October 1818

FAIRIES

Every time a child says 'I don't believe in fairies' there is a little fairy somewhere that falls down dead.
- J.M. Barrie (1860-1937)
  Peter Pan

FAITH

Now faith is the substance of things hoped for, the evidence of things not seen.
- *Bible*, Authorized version
  Hebrews, Ch. 11, v. 1

... he wears his faith but as the fashion of his hat ...
- William Shakespeare (1564-1616)
  Much Ado About Nothing,
  Act I, Sc. I

FAITHFULNESS

Young men want to be faithful, and are not; old men want to be faithless, and cannot.
- Oscar Wilde (1854-1900)
  The Picture of Dorian Gray

FAME

Fame, like water, bears up the lighter things, and lets the weighty sink.
- Pedro Calderón de la Barca
  (1600-81)
  Adventures of Five Hours

... his fame was *noised* throughout all the country.
- *Bible*, Authorised version,
  Joshua, Ch. 6, v. 27

All Fame is dangerous: Good, bringeth Envy; Bad, Shame.
- Thomas Fuller (1654-1734)
  Gnomologia

A man's great fame must always be measured against the means used to acquire it.
- Duc de La Rochefoucauld
  (1613-80)
  Maxims

Fame is something which must be won; honour only something which must not be lost.
- Arthur Schopenhauer
  (1788-1860)
  Aphorisms on the Wisdom of Life

Fame has also this great drawback, that if we pursue it we must direct our lives in such a way as to please the fancy of men, avoiding what they dislike and seeking what is pleasing

Fame / Faults

to them.
— Benedict Spinoza (1632-77)
  Tractate on the Intellect

FAMILIARITY

Though familiarity may not breed
contempt, it takes off the edge of
admiration.
— William Hazlitt (1778-1830)
  Characteristics

FANATICISM

Fanaticism consists in redoubling
your efforts when you have forgotten
your aim.
— George Santayana (1863-1952)
  *The Life of Reason: Reason
  in Common Sense*

FASHIONABLE

You cannot be both fashionable and
first-rate.
— Logan Pearsall Smith (1854-1946)
  Afterthoughts

FATE

Fate is not an eagle, it creeps like
a rat.
— Elizabeth Bowen (1899-1973)
  The House in Paris

It lies not in our power to love
  or hate,
For will in us is over-rul'd by fate.
— Christopher Marlowe (1564-93)
  Hero and Leander

No man can escape his fate.
— Sophocles (*c.* 495-406 BC)
  Oedipus Coloneus

FATHERS

. . . it is a wise father that knows his
own child.
— William Shakespeare (1564-1616)
  The Merchant of Venice, Act II,
  Sc. II

FAULTS

Her faults were mine — her virtues
were her own.
— Lord Byron (1788-1824)
  Maid of Athens

The greatest of faults, I should say,
is to be conscious of none.
— Thomas Carlyle (1795-1881)
  Heroes and Hero-Worship

Mistrust a subordinate who never
finds fault with his superior.
— John Churton Collins
  (1848-1908)
  Aphorisms

How few there are who have courage
enough to own their Faults, or
resolution enough to mend them!
— Benjamin Franklin (1706-90)
  Poor Richard's Almanack, 1743

A Fault, once denied, is twice
committed.
— Thomas Fuller (1654-1734)
  Gnomologia

Prosperous Men seldom mend their
Faults.

53

– Thomas Fuller
  Ibid.

None of us can stand other people
having the same faults as ourselves.
– Oscar Wilde (1854-1900)
  The Picture of Dorian Gray

FEAR

Yea, though I walk through the
valley of the shadow of death, I
will fear no evil . . .
– *Bible*, Authorised version
  Psalms, Ps. 23, v. 4

He who does not fear death does
not fear threats.
– Pierre Corneille (1606-84)
  Le Cid

Fear is stronger than Love.
– Thomas Fuller (1654-1734)
  Gnomologia

. . . a Prince should inspire fear in
suchwise that if he do not win love
he may escape hate. For a man may
very well be feared and yet not
hated, as will always be the case so
long as he does not inter-meddle with
the property or with the women of
his citizens and subjects.
– Niccolo Machiavelli (1469-1527)
  The Prince

Of all base passions, fear is most
accursed.
– William Shakespeare (1564-1616)
  King Henry VI, Pt. I, Act V, Sc. II

There is only one universal passion:
fear.
– George Bernard Shaw

(1856-1950)
The Man of Destiny

FEBRUARY

. . . February, when the days of
winter seem endless and no amount
of wistful recollecting can bring back
any air of summer . . .
– Shirley Jackson (1920-65)
  Raising Demons

FEELINGS

It is as necessary for the heart to feel
as for the body to be fed.
– Napoleon Bonaparte (1769-1821)
  *Political Aphorisms, Moral and
  Philosophical Thoughts of the
  Emperor Napoleon*, collected by
  Cte. Ate. G. De Liancourt

FICTION

The great characters of fiction live as
truly as the memories of dead men.
For the life after death it is not
necessary that a man or woman
should have lived.
– Samuel Butler (1835-1902)
  Note Books

FIERCE

And though she be but little, she is
fierce.
– William Shakespeare (1564-1616)
  A Midsummer-Night's Dream,
  Act III, Sc. II

FIGHTING

What counts is not necessarily the size of the dog in the fight — it's the size of the fight in the dog.
— Dwight D. Eisenhower
    (1890-1969)
    Address, Republican National
    Committee, USA,
    31 January 1958

Never fight with a man who has nothing to lose.
— Baltasar Gracián (1601-58)
    The Art of Worldly Wisdom

FILM MUSIC

Movie music is noise. It's even more painful than my sciatica.
— Sir Thomas Beecham (1879-1961)
    Time, 24 February 1958

FINALITY

Finality is not the language of politics.
— Benjamin Disraeli (1804-81)
    Speech, House of Commons,
    28 February 1859

FLATTERER

I can't be your Friend, and your Flatterer too.
— Thomas Fuller (1654-1734)
    Gnomologia

FLATTERY

I recommend to you . . . an innocent piece of art — that of flattering people behind their backs, in presence of those who, to make their own court, much more than for your sake, will not fail to repeat, and even amplify, the praise to the party concerned. This is, of all flattery, the most pleasing, and consequently the most effectual.
— Earl of Chesterfield (1694-1773)
    Letter to his son, 22 May 1749

. . . there is no way to guard against flattery but by letting it be seen that you take no offence in hearing the truth: but when everyone is free to tell you the truth, respect falls short. Wherefore a prudent Prince should follow a middle course, by choosing certain discreet men from among his subjects, and allowing them alone free leave to speak their minds on any matter on which he asks their opinion, and on none other. But he ought to ask their opinion on everything, and after hearing what they have to say, should reflect and judge for himself.
— Niccolo Machiavelli (1469-1527)
    The Prince

What really flatters a man is that you think him worth flattering.
— George Bernard Shaw
    (1856-1950)
    John Bull's Other Island, Act IV

Among all the diseases of the mind there is not one more epidemical or more pernicious than the love of flattery.
— Sir Richard Steele (1672-1729)
    The Spectator, 3 December 1711

'Tis an old maxim in the schools,
That flattery's the food of fools;
Yet now and then your men of wit

Will condescend to take a bit.
- Jonathan Swift (1667-1745)
  Cadenus and Vanessa

Love of flattery, in most men, proceeds from the mean opinion they have of themselves; in women, from the contrary.
- Jonathan Swift (1667-1745)
  Thoughts on Various Subjects

FOES

You shall judge of a man by his foes as well as by his friends.
- Joseph Conrad (1857-1924)
  Lord Jim

FOOLS

A fool always finds a bigger fool to admire him.
- Nicolas Boileau (1636-1711)
  L'Art Poétique

Fools are in a terrible, overwhelming majority, all the wide world over.
- Henrik Ibsen (1828-1906)
  An Enemy of the People, Act IV

Ninety-nine per cent of the people in the world are fools and the rest of us are in great danger of contagion.
- Thornton Wilder (1897-1975)
  The Matchmaker, Act I

FORCE

Force is not a remedy.
- John Bright (1811-89)
  Speech, Birmingham, England,
  16 November 1880

Who overcomes
By force, hath overcome but half his foe.
- John Milton (1608-74)
  Paradise Lost

FORTUNE

A great Fortune, in the Hands of a Fool, is a great Misfortune.
- Thomas Fuller (1654-1734)
  Gnomologia

To make a fortune some assistance from fate is essential. Ability alone is insufficient.
- Ihara Saikaku (1642-93)
  The Japanese Family Storehouse; or, The Millionaires' Gospel

FRANCE

France is a dog-hole, and it no more merits
The tread of a man's foot . . .
- William Shakespeare (1564-1616)
  All's Well That Ends Well,
  Act II, Sc. III

FREE ECONOMY

We need a free economy not only for the renewed material prosperity it will bring, but because it is indispensable to individual freedom, human dignity and to a more just, more honest society.
- Margaret Thatcher (1925-   )
  Speech, Zurich Economic Society,
  University of Zurich,
  14 March 1977

FREE SPEECH

Everyone is in favour of free speech.
Hardly a day passes without its being
extolled, but some people's idea of it
is that they are free to say what they
like, but if anyone says anything
back, that is an outrage.
– Sir Winston Churchill
(1874-1965)
Speech, House of Commons,
13 October 1943

The right to be heard does not
automatically include the right to be
taken seriously.
– Hubert H. Humphrey (1911-78)
Speech, National Student
Association, Madison, Wisconsin,
23 August 1965

FREE TRADE

Free trade, one of the greatest
blessings which a government can
confer on a people, is in almost every
country unpopular.
– Lord Macaulay (1800-59)
*Essay on Mitford's History of
Greece*

FREEDOM

But what is Freedom? Rightly
  understood,
A universal licence to be good.
– Hartley Coleridge (1796-1849)
Liberty

For what is freedom, but the
  unfettered use
Of all the powers which God for use
  had given?
– Samuel Taylor Coleridge

(1772-1834)
The Destiny of Nations

This will remain the land of the free
only so long as it is the home of the
brave.
– Elmer Davis (1890-1958)
But We Were Born Free

Only the educated are free.
– Epictetus (*c.* 50-*c.* 120)
Discourses

To deny the freedom of the will is
to make morality impossible.
– J.A. Froude (1818-94)
Calvinism

You should never put on your best
trousers when you go out to fight
for freedom and truth.
– Henrik Ibsen (1828-1906)
An Enemy of the People, Act V

The only freedom which deserves the
name, is that of pursuing our own
good in our own way, so long as we
do not attempt to deprive others of
theirs, or impede their efforts to
obtain it.
– John Stuart Mill (1806-73)
On Liberty

If the teachers of mankind are to be
cognisant of all that they ought to
know, everything must be free to be
written and published without
restraint.
– John Stuart Mill
Ibid.

Give me the liberty to know, to
utter, and to argue freely according
to conscience, above all liberties.
– John Milton (1608-74)
Areopagitica

Freedom / Frenchmen / Friends

Man was born free, and everywhere
he is in chains.
- Jean Jacques Rousseau (1712-78)
  Du Contrat Social

FRENCHMEN

The Almighty in his infinite wisdom
did not see fit to create Frenchmen
in the image of Englishmen.
- Sir Winston Churchill
  (1874-1965)
  Speech, House of Commons,
  10 December 1942

The Frenchman, easy, debonair,
  and brisk,
Give him his lass, his fiddle, and
  his frisk,
Is always happy, reign whoever may.
- William Cowper (1731-1800)
  Table Talk

FRIENDS

Friends are born, not made.
- Henry Brooks Adams
  (1838-1918)
  The Education of Henry Adams

A friend in power is a friend lost.
- Henry Brooks Adams
  Ibid.

One friend in a lifetime is much; two
are many; three are hardly possible.
- Henry Brooks Adams
  Ibid.

Business, you know, may bring
money, but friendship hardly ever
does.

- Jane Austen (1775-1817)
  Emma

A friend loveth at all times, and a
brother is born for adversity.
- *Bible*, Authorized version
  Proverbs, Ch. 17, v. 17

Friendship is like money, easier
made than kept.
- Samuel Butler (1835-1902)
  Note Books

A woman can become a man's friend
only in the following stages – first an
acquaintance, next a mistress, and
only then a friend.
- Anton Chekhov (1860-1904)
  Uncle Vanya, Act II

Remember to make a great difference
between companions and friends; for
a very complaisant and agreeable
companion may, and very often does,
prove a very improper and a very
dangerous friend.
- Earl of Chesterfield (1694-1773)
  Letter to his son, 9 October 1747

A friend may well be reckoned the
masterpiece of Nature.
- Ralph Waldo Emerson (1803-82)
  Essays: Friendship

Nothing can come between true
friends.
- Euripides (*c.* 485-406 BC)
  Hercules Furens

An open Foe may prove a curse;
But a pretended friend is worse.
- Benjamin Franklin (1706-90)
  Poor Richard's Almanack, 1740

A true Friend is the best Possession.
– Benjamin Franklin (1706-90)
Poor Richard's Almanack, 1744

A Friend is never known till needed.
– Thomas Fuller (1654-1734)
Gnomologia

'Tis easier to preserve a Friend, than to recover him when lost.
– Thomas Fuller
Ibid.

'Tis almost as easy to find a true Diamond, as a true Friend.
– Thomas Fuller
Ibid.

He that ceaseth to be a Friend, never was a good one.
– Thomas Fuller
Ibid.

A Friend, that you buy with Presents, will be bought from you.
– Thomas Fuller,
Ibid.

A rich Friend is a Treasure.
– Thomas Fuller
Ibid.

In times of Prosperity Friends will be plenty.
In time of Adversity not one in twenty.
– Thomas Fuller
Ibid.

Friendships multiply Joys, and divide Grief.
– Thomas Fuller
Ibid.

Friendship is a disinterested commerce between equals; love, an abject intercourse between tyrants and slaves.
– Oliver Goldsmith (1728-74)
The Good-Natured Man

We often choose a friend as we do a mistress – for no particular excellence in themselves, but merely from some circumstance that flatters our self-love.
– William Hazlitt (1778-1830)
Characteristics

He will never have true friends who is afraid of making enemies.
– William Hazlitt
Ibid.

Friendship, like credit, is highest where it is not used.
– Elbert Hubbard (1856-1915)
The Note Book

True love may be rare, but true friendship is even rarer.
– Duc de La Rochefoucauld (1613-80)
Maxims

Friends are like melons. Shall I tell you why?
To find one good, you must a hundred try.
– Claude Mermet (1550?-1605)
Epigram on Friends

Most friendship is feigning, most loving mere folly.
– William Shakespeare (1564-1616)
As You Like It, Act II, Sc. VII

My friends were poor, but honest.
– William Shakespeare (1564-1616)
All's Well That Ends Well,
Act I, Sc. III

FUN

I've taken my fun where I've found it;
I've rogued an' I've ranged in my
  time.
− Rudyard Kipling (1865-1936)
   The Ladies

FUNNY

Funny peculiar, or funny ha-ha?
− Ian Hay (1876-1952)
   Housemaster

FURY

Beware the fury of a patient man.
− John Dryden (1631-1700)
   Absalom and Achitophel

FUTURE

If you do not think about the future,
you cannot have one.
− John Galsworthy (1867-1933)
   Swan Song

If you want a picture of the future,
imagine a boot stamping on a human
face − for ever.
− George Orwell (1903-50)
   1984

GENERALIZATIONS

All generalizations are false, including
this one.
− Alexander Chase (1926-   )
   Perspectives

Generalization is necessary to the
advancement of knowledge; but

particularity is indispensable to the
creations of the imagination.
− Lord Macaulay (1800-59)
   Milton

GENERATIONS

The existing generation is master
both of the training and the entire
circumstances of the generation to
come . . .
− John Stuart Mill (1806-73)
   On Liberty

Every generation revolts against its
fathers and makes friends with its
grandfathers.
− Lewis Mumford (1895-   )
   The Brown Decades

The old believe everything; the
middle-aged suspect everything; the
young know everything.
− Oscar Wilde (1854-1900)
   'Phrases and Philosophies for the
   Use of the Young', *Chameleon*,
   December, 1894

GENIUS

Since when was genius found
respectable?
− Elizabeth Barrett Browning
   (1806-61)
   Aurora Leigh

A harmless hilarity, and a buoyant
cheerfulness are not infrequent
concomitants of genius; and we are
never more deceived, than when we
mistake gravity for greatness,
solemnity for science, and pomposity
for erudition.
− Reverend C.C. Colton

(1780?-1832)
Lacon

A fine genius in his own country, is like gold in the mine.
— Benjamin Franklin (1706-90)
  Poor Richard's Almanack, 1733

Genius, in truth, means little more than the faculty of perceiving in an unhabitual way.
— William James (1842-1910)
  The Principles of Psychology

Everyone is a genius at least once a year. The real geniuses simply have their bright ideas closer together.
— Georg Christoph Lichtenberg
  (1742-99)
  Aphorisms

Persons of genius, it is true, are, and are always likely to be, a small minority; but in order to have them, it is necessary to preserve the soil in which they grow. Genius can only breathe freely in an *atmosphere* of freedom.
— John Stuart Mill (1806-73)
  On Liberty

There is no great genius without a touch of madness.
— Seneca (*c*. 4 BC-65 AD)
  De Tranquilitate Animi

When a true genius appears in the world, you may know him by this sign, that the dunces are all in confederacy against him.
— Jonathan Swift (1667-1745)
  Thoughts on Various Subjects

. . . Genius lasts longer than Beauty.
— Oscar Wilde (1854-1900)
  The Picture of Dorian Gray

GENTEEL MANNER

However trifling a genteel manner may sound, it is of very great consequence towards pleasing in private life, especially the women . . .
— Earl of Chesterfield (1694-1773)
  Letter to his son, 25 July 1741

GENTLEMEN

Money and good Manners make the Gentleman.
— Benjamin Franklin (1706-90)
  Poor Richard's Almanack, 1742

Manners and Money make a Gentleman.
— Thomas Fuller (1654-1734)
  Gnomologia

I am a gentleman: I live by robbing the poor.
— George Bernard Shaw
  (1856-1950)
  Man and Superman, Act III

The only infallible rule we know is, that the man who is always talking about being a gentleman never is one.
— R.S. Surtees (1803-64)
  Ask Mamma

He was a gentleman who was generally spoken of as having nothing a-year, paid quarterly.
— R.S. Surtees (1803-64)
  Mr Sponge's Sporting Tour

GHOST

Ghost, n. The outward and visible sign of an inward fear.
— Ambrose Bierce

61

(1842-1914?)
The Devil's Dictionary

GIVING

It is more blessed to give than to receive.
— *Bible*, Authorized version
  Acts, Ch. 20, v. 35

GLORY

The paths of glory lead but to the grave.
— Thomas Gray (1716-71)
  Elegy Written in a Country Churchyard

GOD

GOD *is* our refuge and strength, a very present help in trouble.
— *Bible*, Authorized version
  Psalms, Ps. 46, v. 1

God is a respecter of persons — no one more so.
— Samuel Butler (1835-1902)
  Note Books

God moves in a mysterious way His wonders to perform.
— William Cowper (1731-1800)
  Olney Hymns

God helps them that help themselves.
— Benjamin Franklin (1706-90)
  Poor Richard's Almanack, 1736

God and all the attributes of God are eternal.
— Benedict Spinoza (1632-77)
  Ethics

If God did not exist, it would be necessary to invent him.
— Voltaire (1694-1778)
  Épîtres

GOLDEN AGE

The golden Age never was the present Age.
— Thomas Fuller (1654-1734)
  Gnomologia

Those who compare the age in which their lot has fallen with a golden age which exists only in imagination, may talk of degeneracy and decay; but no man who is correctly informed as to the past will be disposed to take a morose or desponding view of the present.
— Lord Macaulay (1800-59)
  History of England

GOLDEN RULE

The golden rule is that there are no golden rules.
— George Bernard Shaw (1856-1950)
  Man and Superman: Maxims for Revolutionists

GOOD

It is not enough to do good; one must do it the right way.
— Lord Morley (Viscount Morley of Blackburn) (1838-1923)
  Rousseau

. . . for there is nothing either good or bad, but thinking makes it so . . .
— William Shakespeare

(1564-1616)
Hamlet, Act II, Sc. 2

Reflections on the Revolution in France

GOOD BREEDING

Good breeding consists in concealing how much we think of ourselves and how little we think of the other person.
— Mark Twain (1835-1910)
  Notebooks

GOOD LUCK

It is a very bad thing to become accustomed to good luck.
— Publilius Syrus
  (*c.* 1st century BC)
  Maxims

GOOD MANNERS

Good manners have much to do with the emotions. To make them ring true, one must feel them, not merely exhibit them.
— Amy Vanderbilt (1908-74)
  New Complete Book of Etiquette

GOOD NEWS

As cold waters to a thirsty soul, so *is* good news from a far country.
— *Bible*, Authorized version
  Proverbs, Ch. 25, v. 25

GOOD ORDER

Good order is the foundation of all good things.
— Edmund Burke (1729-97)

GOOD SENSE

Good Sense is a Thing all need, few have, and none think they want.
— Benjamin Franklin (1706-90)
  Poor Richard's Almanack, 1746

GOODNESS

Goodness without wisdom always accomplishes evil.
— Robert A. Heinlein (1907-   )
  Stranger in a Strange Land

Very rarely do Men know how to be either Wholly Good or Wholly Bad.
— Niccolo Machiavelli (1469-1527)
  Discourses

GOSSIP

Gossip is a sort of smoke that comes from the dirty tobacco-pipes of those who diffuse it; it proves nothing but the bad taste of the smoker.
— George Eliot (1819-80)
  Daniel Deronda

There is only one thing in the world worse than being talked about, and that is not being talked about.
— Oscar Wilde (1854-1900)
  The Picture of Dorian Gray

GOVERNMENT

Fear is the foundation of most governments.

Government

- John Adams (1735-1826)
  Thoughts on Government

The worst thing in the world, next to anarchy, is government.
- Henry Ward Beecher (1813-87)
  Proverbs from Plymouth Pulpit

It is with government as with medicine. Its only business is the choice of evils. Every law is an evil, for every law is an infraction of liberty.
- Jeremy Bentham (1748-1832)
  Principles of Legislation

Government is a contrivance of human wisdom to provide for human wants.
- Edmund Burke (1729-97)
  Reflections on the Revolution in France

Democracy means government by the uneducated, while aristocracy means government by the badly educated.
- G.K. Chesterton (1874-1936)
  New York Times,
  1 February 1931

Every new administration, not excluding ourselves, arrives in power with bright and benevolent ideas of using public money to do good. The more frequent the changes of government, the more numerous are the bright ideas, and the more frequent the elections, the more benevolent they become.
- Sir Winston Churchill
  (1874-1965)
  Speech, House of Commons,
  11 April 1927

I believe that without party Parliamentary government is impossible.
- Benjamin Disraeli (1804-81)
  Speech, Manchester, 3 April 1872

No Government can be long secure without a formidable Opposition.
- Benjamin Disraeli (1804-81)
  Coningsby

The less government we have, the better – the fewer laws, and the less confided power.
- Ralph Waldo Emerson (1803-82)
  Essays: Politics

Those who govern, having much business on their hands, do not generally like to take the trouble of considering and carrying into execution new projects. The best public measures are therefore seldom adopted from previous wisdom, but forced by the occasion.
- Benjamin Franklin (1706-90)
  Autobiography

. . . *all* government, whatever its forms or pretenses, is a dead weight that paralyzes the free spirit and activities of the masses.
- Emma Goldman (1869-1940)
  My Disillusionment in Russia

Nothing appears more surprising to those who consider human affairs with a philosophical eye, than the easiness with which the many are governed by the few.
- David Hume (1711-76)
  First Principles of Government

Every country has the government it deserves.
- Joseph de Maistre (1753-1821)
  Lettres et Opuscules Inédits,
  15 August 1811

He who governs should possess
energy without fanaticism, principles
without demagogy, severity without
cruelty; he must neither be weak, nor
vacillating, nor, so to express it,
must he be ashamed to do his duty.
— Napoleon Bonaparte (1769-1821)
  *Political Aphorisms, Moral and
  Philosophical Thoughts of the
  Emperor Napoleon*, collected by
  Cte. Ate. G. De Liancourt

Governments arise either out of the
people or over the people.
— Thomas Paine (1737-1809)
  The Rights of Man

. . . Government, even in its best
state, is but a necessary evil; in its
worst state, an intolerable one.
— Thomas Paine (1737-1809)
  Common Sense

Fear and hope are the two great
instruments for the governance of
men . . .
— Jean Jacques Rousseau (1712-78)
  Projet Pour La Corse

That government is best which
governs least.
— Henry David Thoreau (1817-62)
  Civil Disobedience

Governments perish usually through
impotence or tyranny. In the first
case power eludes them; in the
second it is seized from them.
— Alexis de Tocqueville (1805-59)
  Democracy in America

In general, the art of government
consists in taking as much money as
possible from one class of citizens
to give to the other.

— Voltaire (1694-1778)
  Dictionnaire Philosophique

GOVERNMENT EXPENDITURE

Thrift should be the guiding principle
in our government expenditure. It
should be made clear to all
government workers that corruption
and waste are very great crimes.
— Mao Tse-tung (1893-1976)
  Our Economic Policy,
  23 January 1934

GRATITUDE

Gratitude preserves old Friendship,
and procures new.
— Thomas Fuller (1654-1734)
  Gnomologia

GREAT MEN

Great men are not *always* wise:
neither do the aged understand
judgment.
— *Bible*, Authorized version
  Job, Ch. 32, v. 9

Nothing great will ever be achieved
without great men, and men are great
only if they are determined to be so.
— Charles de Gaulle (1890-1970)
  Le Fil de L'Épée

The world's great men have not
commonly been great scholars, nor
great scholars great men.
— Oliver Wendell Holmes (1809-94)
  The Chambered Nautilus

Great Men / Guests

Ambition and the enjoyment of high offices, do not constitute the happiness and satisfaction of a great man; he seeks the good opinion of the world and the esteem of posterity.
— Napoleon Bonaparte (1769-1821)
   Political Aphorisms, Moral and Philosophical Thoughts of the Emperor Napoleon, collected by Cte. Ate. G. De Liancourt

GREAT MINDS

Great Minds and great Fortunes don't always go together.
— Thomas Fuller (1654-1734)
   Gnomologia

GREATNESS

To be great is to be misunderstood.
— Ralph Waldo Emerson (1803-82)
   Essays: Self-Reliance

. . . be not afraid of greatness: some are born great, some achieve greatness, and some have greatness thrust upon 'em.
— William Shakespeare (1564-1616)
   Twelfth Night, Act II, Sc. V

GREEK

I am not of the opinion generally entertained in this country, that man lives by Greek and Latin alone; that is, by knowing a great many words of two dead languages, which nobody knows perfectly, and which are of no use in the common intercourse of life.
— Earl of Chesterfield (1694-1773)
   Letter to Mrs Eugenia Stanhope, 5 November 1769

GREENHOUSES

Who loves a garden loves a greenhouse too.
— William Cowper (1731-1800)
   The Task: The Garden

GRIEF

Grief drives men into habits of serious reflection, sharpens the understanding and softens the heart.
— John Adams (1735-1826)
   Letter to Thomas Jefferson, 6 May 1816

Grief is itself a med'cine.
— William Cowper (1731-1800)
   Charity

The bitterest tears shed over graves are for words left unsaid and deeds left undone.
— Harriet Beecher Stowe (1811-96)
   Little Foxes

GRIEVANCE

To have a grievance is to have a purpose in life.
— Eric Hoffer (1902-   )
   The Passionate State of Mind

GUESTS

To be an ideal guest, stay at home.
— Edgar Watson Howe (1853-1937)
   Country Town Sayings

HABITS

Curious things, habits. People themselves never knew they had them.
— Agatha Christie (1890-1976)
  Witness for the Prosecution

Who is strong? He that can conquer his bad Habits.
— Benjamin Franklin (1706-90)
  Poor Richard's Almanack, 1744

'Tis easier to prevent bad habits than to break them.
— Benjamin Franklin
  Ibid., 1745

It is easier to prevent ill Habits, than to brake them.
— Thomas Fuller (1654-1734)
  Gnomologia

Habit is stronger than reason.
— George Santayana (1863-1952)
  Interpretations of Poetry and Religion

HAIR

. . . if a woman have long hair, it is a glory to her . . .
— *Bible*, Authorized version
  I Corinthians, Ch11, v. 15

HAPPINESS

Happiness depends upon ourselves.
— Aristotle (384-322 BC)
  Nicomachean Ethics

Perfect happiness, even in memory, is not common.
— Jane Austen (1775-1817)
  Emma

A large income is the best recipe for happiness I ever heard of.
— Jane Austen (1775-1817)
  Mansfield Park

Happy *is* the man *that* findeth wisdom, and the man *that* getteth understanding.
— *Bible*, Authorized version
  Proverbs, Ch. 3, v. 13

People don't notice whether it's winter or summer when they're happy.
— Anton Chekhov (1860-1904)
  Three Sisters, Act II

Happiness is a mystery like religion, and should never be rationalized.
— G.K. Chesterton (1874-1936)
  Heretics

If kings would only determine not to extend their dominions, until they had filled them with happiness, they would find the smallest territories too large, but the longest life too short, for the full accomplishment of so grand and so noble an ambition.
— Reverend C.C. Colton
  (1780?-1832)
  Lacon

Happiness lies in the fulfilment of the spirit through the body.
— Cyril Connolly (1903-74)
  The Unquiet Grave

Let him who would be happy for a day, go to the barber; for a week, marry a wife; for a month, buy him a new horse; for a year, build him a new house; for all his life time, be an

Happiness

honest man.
- Thomas Fuller (1608-61)
  *The History of the Worthies
  of England*

Happiness generally depends more on
the Opinion we have of Things, than
on the Things themselves.
- Thomas Fuller (1654-1734)
  Gnomologia

The search for happiness is one of the
chief sources of unhappiness.
- Eric Hoffer (1902-   )
  The Passionate State of Mind

The supreme happiness of life is the
conviction that we are loved.
- Victor Hugo (1802-85)
  Les Misérables

A man's happiness or unhappiness
depends as much on his temperament
as on his destiny.
- Duc de La Rochefoucauld
  (1613-80)
  Maxims

A sound mind in a sound body, is a
short but full description of a happy
state in this world. He that has these
two, has little more to wish for; and
he that wants either of them, will be
little the better for anything else.
- John Locke (1632-1704)
  *Some Thoughts Concerning
  Education*

The first requisite for the happiness
of the people is the abolition of
religion.
- Karl Marx (1818-83)
  *A Criticism of the Hegelian
  Philosophy of Right*

Ask yourself whether you are happy,
and you cease to be so.
- John Stuart Mill (1806-73)
  Autobiography

A being of higher faculties requires
more to make him happy, is capable
probably of more acute suffering,
and certainly accessible to it at more
points, than one of an inferior type;
but in spite of these liabilities, he can
never really wish to sink into what he
feels to be a lower grade of existence.
- John Stuart Mill (1806-73)
  Utilitarianism

It is indisputable that the being
whose capacities of enjoyment are
low, has the greatest chance of having
them fully satisfied; and a highly
endowed being will always feel that
any happiness which he can look for,
as the world is constituted, is
imperfect.
- John Stuart Mill (1806-73)
  Ibid.

Happiness is a by-product of an
effort to make someone else happy.
- Gretta Brooker Palmer (1905-53)
  Permanent Marriage

No man is happy unless he believes
he is.
- Publilius Syrus
  (*c.* 1st century BC)
  Maxims

A lifetime of happiness: no man alive
could bear it: it would be hell on
earth.
- George Bernard Shaw
  (1856-1950)
  Man and Superman, Act I

We have no more right to consume happiness without producing it than to consume wealth without producing it.
— George Bernard Shaw (1856-1950)
  Candida, Act I

We are never happy: we can only remember that we were so once.
— Alexander Smith (1830-67)
  Dreamthorp

Happiness is no laughing matter.
— Richard Whately (1787-1863)
  Apophthegms

A man can be happy with any woman, as long as he does not love her.
— Oscar Wilde (1854-1900)
  The Picture of Dorian Gray

HARANGUE

Harangue, n. A speech by an opponent, who is known as an harangue-outang.
— Ambrose Bierce (1842-1914?)
  The Devil's Dictionary

HARD TIMES

Can anybody remember when the times were not hard and money not scarce?
— Ralph Waldo Emerson (1803-82)
  Society and Solitude

HASTE

Haste in every business brings failures.

— Herodotus (*c.* 485-*c.* 425 BC)
  The Histories of Herodotus

HATE

Let them hate so long as they fear.
— Lucius Accius (170-90 BC)
  Atreus

I tell you there is such a thing as creative hate!
— Willa Cather (1873-1947)
  The Song of the Lark

Love, friendship, respect, do not unite people as much as a common hatred for something.
— Anton Chekhov (1860-1904)
  Note Books

They hate whom they fear.
— Ennius (239-169 BC)
  Thyestes

Those who are fear'd, are hated.
— Benjamin Franklin (1706-90)
  Poor Richard's Almanack, 1744

HEADMASTERS

Headmasters have powers at their disposal with which Prime Ministers have never yet been invested.
— Sir Winston Churchill (1874-1965)
  My Early Life

HEALTH

Health and cheerfulness mutually beget each other.
— Joseph Addison (1672-1719)
  The Spectator, 24 May 1712

He who hath good health is young.
- Henry George Bohn (1796-1884)
  Handbook of Proverbs

Thousands upon thousands of persons have studied disease. Almost no one has studied health.
- Adelle Davis (1904-74)
  Let's Eat Right to Keep Fit

Health is infectious.
- Georg Christoph Lichtenberg (1742-99)
  Aphorisms

The preservation of health is a duty. Few seem conscious that there is such a thing as physical morality.
- Herbert Spencer (1820-1903)
  Education

HEART-BREAK

There were many ways of breaking a heart. Stories were full of hearts being broken by love, but what really broke a heart was taking away its dream – whatever that dream might be.
- Pearl S. Buck (1892-1973)
  The Patriot

HEIGHT

Well, I'm about as tall as a shotgun, and just as noisy.
- Truman Capote (1924-   )
  Time, 3 March 1952

HEIRESSES

All heiresses are beautiful.
- John Dryden (1631-1700)
  King Arthur, Act I

HELL

Believing in Hell must distort every judgement on this life.
- Cyril Connolly (1903-74)
  The Unquiet Grave

Hell is a city much like London –
A populous and smoky city.
- Percy Bysshe Shelley (1792-1822)
  Peter Bell the Third

HELP

The gods help them that help themselves.
- Aesop (*c.* 550 BC)
  Fables: Hercules and the Waggoner

But what is past my help is past my care.
- Francis Beaumont (1584-1616) and John Fletcher (1579-1625)
  The Double Marriage, Act I

HERESY

Heresy is the lifeblood of religions. It is faith that begets heretics. There are no heresies in a dead religion.
- André Suarès (1868-1948)
  Péguy

HEROES

Every hero becomes a bore at last.
- Ralph Waldo Emerson (1803-82)
  Representative Men: Uses of Great Men

HIDE

Love, the Itch, and a Cough cannot
be hid.
— Thomas Fuller (1654-1734)
  Gnomologia

HIERARCHIES

In a hierarchy, every employee tends
to rise to his level of incompetence.
— Laurence Peter (1919-   )
  The Peter Principle

HIGHBROW

A highbrow is a person educated
beyond his intelligence.
— James Brander Matthews
  (1852-1929)
  Epigrams

HISTORIANS

The historian, essentially, wants more
documents than he can really use; the
dramatist only wants more liberties
than he can really take.
— Henry James (1843-1916)
  The Aspern Papers

The historian is a prophet in reverse.
— Friedrich von Schlegel
  (1772-1829)
  Athenaeum

HISTORY

History, n. An account mostly false,
of events mostly unimportant, which
are brought about by rulers mostly
knaves, and soldiers mostly fools.

— Ambrose Bierce (1842-1914?)
  The Devil's Dictionary

No great man lives in vain. The
history of the world is but the
biography of great men.
— Thomas Carlyle (1795-1881)
  *Heroes and Hero Worship: The
  Hero as Divinity*

History is more or less bunk. It's
tradition. We don't want tradition.
We want to live in the present and
the only history that is worth a
tinker's damn is the history we make
today.
— Henry Ford (1863-1947)
  Chicago Tribune, 25 May 1916

My argument is that War makes
rattling good history; but Peace is
poor reading.
— Thomas Hardy (1840-1928)
  The Dynasts

What experience and history teach is
this — that people and governments
never have learned anything from
history, or acted on principles
deduced from it.
— Georg Wilhelm Friedrich Hegel
  (1770-1831)
  Philosophy of History

The history of all hitherto existing
society is the history of class
struggles.
— Karl Marx (1818-83) and
  Friedrich Engels (1820-95)
  The Communist Manifesto

The history of the world is the
history of a privileged few.
— Henry Miller (1891-1980)
  Sunday After the War

History has nothing to record save wars and revolutions: the peaceful years appear only as brief pauses or interludes, scattered here and there.
— Arthur Schopenhauer (1788-1860)
Parerga and Paralipomena

We learn from history that we learn nothing from history.
— George Bernard Shaw (1856-1950)
Man and Superman: The Revolutionist's Handbook

Human history becomes more and more a race between education and catastrophe.
— H.G. Wells (1866-1946)
The Outline of History

Human history is in essence a history of ideas.
— H.G. Wells
Ibid.

The one duty we owe to history is to re-write it.
— Oscar Wilde (1854-1900)
The Critic as Artist

. . . history is nothing more than a tableau of crimes and misfortunes.
— Voltaire (1694-1778)
L'Ingénu

HOLLYWOOD

Hollywood always had a streak of the totalitarian in just about everything it did.
— Shirley MacLaine (1934-   )
You Can Get There from Here

HOME

A man's home is his wife's castle.
— Alexander Chase (1926-   )
Perspe·tives

Home is the place where, when you have to go there,
They have to take you in.
— Robert Frost (1874-1963)
The Death of the Hired Man

Home is the girl's prison and the woman's workhouse.
— George Bernard Shaw (1856-1950)
Man and Superman: Maxims for Revolutionists

HONESTY

It is not the interest of honesty or talent or virtue, but that of health and happiness that should take the highest place. Honesty is made for happiness, not happiness for honesty.
— Samuel Butler (1835-1902)
Note Books

He that loseth his honesty, hath nothing else to lose.
— John Lyly (1554?-1606)
Euphues: Euphues and Eubulus

An honest Man's the noblest work of God.
— Alexander Pope (1688-1744)
An Essay on Man

. . . no legacy is so rich as honesty.
— William Shakespeare (1564-1616)
All's Well That Ends Well,
Act III, Sc. V

HONEYMOONS

I think that most wearisome
institution, the honeymoon, must
have been inaugurated by some
sworn foe to matrimony, some vile
misogynist, who took himself a wife
in order to discover, by experience,
the best mode of rendering married
life a martyrdom.
— Mary Elizabeth Braddon
    (1837-1915)
    Dead-Sea Fruit

HONOUR

Why do men seek honour? Surely in
order to confirm the favourable
opinion they have formed of
themselves.
— Aristotle (384-322 BC)
    Nicomachean Ethics

The louder he talked of his honour,
the faster we counted our spoons.
— Ralph Waldo Emerson (1803-82)
    Conduct of Life: Worship

Honour is flashed off exploit.
— Gerard Manley Hopkins
    (1844-89)
    St Alphonsus Rodriguez

HOPE

Hope is a good breakfast, but it is a
bad supper.
— Francis Bacon (1561-1626)
    Apothegms

He that lives upon Hope, dies farting.
— Benjamin Franklin (1706-90)
    Poor Richard's Almanack, 1736

Great Hopes make great Men.
— Thomas Fuller (1654-1734)
    Gnomologia

Hope is as cheap as Despair.
— Thomas Fuller
    Ibid.

Hope springs eternal in the human
breast.
— Alexander Pope (1688-1744)
    An Essay on Man

Extreme hopes are born of extreme
misery.
— Bertrand Russell (1872-1970)
    *Unpopular Essays: The Future
    of Mankind*

The miserable have no other medicine
But only hope.
— William Shakespeare (1564-1616)
    Measure for Measure,
    Act III, Sc. I

HORRIBLE

There is but one step from the
grotesque to the horrible.
— Sir Arthur Conan Doyle
    (1859-1930)
    His Last Bow: Wisteria Lodge

HOTELS

It is because we put up with bad
things that hotel-keepers continue
to give them to us.
— Anthony Trollope (1815-82)
    Orley Farm

HOUSE OF LORDS

We in the House of Lords are never in touch with public opinion. That makes us a civilized body.
- Oscar Wilde (1854-1900)
  A Woman of No Importance,
  Act I

HOUSES

Houses are built to live in, and not to look on.
- Francis Bacon (1561-1626)
  Essays: Of Building

A man builds a fine house; and now he has a master, and a task for life: he is to furnish, watch, show it, and keep it in repair, the rest of his days.
- Ralph Waldo Emerson (1803-82)
  Society and Solitude:
  Works and Days

A house without woman and firelight, is like a body without soul or sprite.
- Benjamin Franklin (1706-90)
  Poor Richard's Almanack, 1733

No house should ever be *on* any hill or on anything. It should be *of* the hill, belonging to it, so hill and house could live together each the happier for the other.
- Frank Lloyd Wright (1869-1959)
  An Autobiography

HUMAN NATURE

There is in human nature generally more of the fool than of the wise.
- Francis Bacon (1561-1626)
  Essays: Of Boldness

Human nature is not a machine to be built after a model, and set to do exactly the work prescribed for it, but a tree, which requires to grow and develop itself on all sides, according to the tendency of the inward forces which make it a living thing.
- John Stuart Mill (1806-73)
  On Liberty

Two Principles in human nature reign; Self-love, to urge, and Reason, to
  restrain.
- Alexander Pope (1688-1744)
  An Essay on Man

HUMAN SPECIES

The human species, according to the best theory I can form of it, is composed of two distinct races, *the men who borrow*, and *the men who lend*.
- Charles Lamb (1775-1834)
  Essays of Elia: The Two Races of Men

HUMILIATION

Nothing is more humiliating than to see idiots succeed in enterprises we have failed in.
- Gustave Flaubert (1821-80)
  Sentimental Education

HUMOUR

A sense of humour keen enough to show a man his own absurdities as well as those of other people will keep a man from the commission of all sins, or nearly all, save those that

are worth committing.
— Samuel Butler (1835-1902)
Note Books

Men will confess to treason, murder, arson, false teeth, or a wig. How many of them will own up to a lack of humor?
— Frank Colby (1865-1925)
Essays

Humour brings insight and tolerance.
— Agnes Repplier (1858-1950)
In Pursuit of Laughter

HUNGER

The best sauce in the world is hunger.
— Miguel de Cervantes (1547-1616)
Don Quixote

HUNTING

The English country gentleman galloping after a fox — the unspeakable in full pursuit of the uneatable.
— Oscar Wilde (1854-1900)
A Woman of No Importance,
Act I

HURT

The moral rules which forbid mankind to hurt one another (in which we must never forget to include wrongful interference with each other's freedom) are more vital to human well-being than any maxims, however important, which only point out the best mode of managing some department of human affairs.

— John Stuart Mill (1806-73)
Utilitarianism

HUSBANDS

It is necessary to be almost a genius to make a good husband.
— Honoré de Balzac (1799-1850)
Physiology of Marriage

Being a husband is a whole-time job. That is why so many husbands fail. They cannot give their entire attention to it.
— Arnold Bennett (1867-1931)
The Title, Act I

A good husband makes a good wife.
— Robert Burton (1577-1640)
Anatomy of Melancholy

There is no creature perfectly civil but a husband. For in a little time he grows only rude to his wife, and this is the highest good breeding, for it begets his civility to other people.
— William Congreve (1670-1729)
Love for Love, Act I

A husband is what is left of the lover after the nerve has been extracted.
— Helen Rowland (1876-1950)
The Rubaiyat of a Bachelor

Before marriage, a man declares that he would lay down his life to serve you; after marriage, he won't even lay down his newspaper to talk to you.
— Helen Rowland (1876-1950)
A Guide to Men

75

Ideas / Imagination

IDEAS

One of the greatest pains to human
nature is the pain of a new idea.
– Walter Bagehot (1826-77)
   Physics and Politics

Our ideas are for the most part like
bad sixpences, and we spend our
lives in trying to pass them on one
another.
– Samuel Butler (1835-1902)
   Note Books

Every new idea has something of the
pain and peril of childbirth about it.
– Samuel Butler
   Ibid.

Ideas of all kinds, serviceable and the
reverse, are like mushroom spawn,
always in the air, and catch on to the
minds most fitted to receive them.
– Samuel Butler
   Ibid.

Ideas and opinions, like living
organisms, have a normal rate of
growth which cannot be either
checked or forced beyond a certain
point.
– Samuel Butler
   Ibid.

No grand idea was ever born in a
conference, but a lot of foolish ideas
have died there.
– F. Scott Fitzgerald (1896-1940)
   The Crack-up

All great ideas are dangerous.
– Oscar Wilde (1854-1900)
   De Profundis

IDEALISTS

An idealist is one who, on noticing
that a rose smells better than a
cabbage, concludes that it will also
make better soup.
– H.L. Mencken (1880-1956)
   Chrestomathy

IDEALS

Ideals are dangerous things. Realities
are better. They wound, but they're
better.
– Oscar Wilde (1854-1900)
   Lady Windermere's Fan, Act IV

If I lost my ideals, I should lose
everything.
– Oscar Wilde
   Ibid., Act IV

ILLUSIONS

Don't part with your illusions. When
they are gone, you may still exist,
but you have ceased to live.
– Mark Twain (1835-1910)
   Pudd'nhead Wilson's Calendar

IMAGINATION

A lady's imagination is very rapid; it
jumps from admiration to love, from
love to matrimony in a moment.
– Jane Austen (1775-1817)
   Pride and Prejudice

The imagination is the secret and
marrow of civilization.
– Henry Ward Beecher (1813-87)
   Proverbs from Plymouth Pulpit

Imagination / Inaction

Imagination is more important than knowledge.
– Albert Einstein (1879-1955)
   On Science

The imagination of a boy is healthy, and the mature imagination of a man is healthy; but there is a space of life between, in which the soul is in a ferment, the character undecided, the way of life uncertain, the ambition thick-sighted: thence proceeds mawkishness.
– John Keats (1795-1821)
   Endymion: Preface

I am certain of nothing but of the holiness of the Heart's affections and the truth of Imagination – What the imagination seizes as Beauty must be truth – whether it existed before or not.
– John Keats (1795-1821)
   Letter to Benjamin Bailey,
   22 November 1817

Imagination grows by exercise and contrary to common belief is more powerful in the mature than in the young.
– Somerset Maugham (1874-1965)
   The Summing Up

IMITATION

Imitation is the sincerest form of flattery.
– Reverend C.C. Colton
   (1780?-1832)
   Lacon

There is much difference between imitating a good man, and counterfeiting him.

– Benjamin Franklin (1706-90)
   Poor Richard's Almanack, 1738

IMPARTIAL

Impartial, adj. Unable to perceive any promise of personal advantage from espousing either side of a controversy or adopting either of two conflicting opinions.
– Ambrose Bierce (1842-1914?)
   The Devil's Dictionary

IMPORTANT

A thing is important if anyone *think* it important.
– William James (1842-1910)
   The Principles of Psychology

IMPROBABLE

One should always be a little improbable.
– Oscar Wilde (1854-1900)
   'Phrases and Philosophies for the
   Use of the Young', *Chameleon*,
   December, 1894

INACTION

A person may cause evil to others not only by his actions but by his inaction, and in either case he is justly accountable to them for the injury.
– John Stuart Mill (1806-73)
   On Liberty

INCOMPATIBILITY

Incompatibility, n. In matrimony a
similarity of tastes, particularly the
taste for domination.
- Ambrose Bierce (1842-1914?)
  The Devil's Dictionary

INDECISION

There is no more miserable human
being than one in whom nothing is
habitual but indecision.
- William James (1842-1910)
  The Principles of Psychology

INDEPENDENCE

To be poor and independent is very
nearly an impossibility.
- William Cobbett (1762-1835)
  Advice to Young Men

The first of earthly blessings,
independence.
- Edward Gibbon (1737-94)
  Autobiography

It's easy to be independent when
you've got money. But to be
independent when you haven't got a
thing — that's the Lord's test.
- Mahalia Jackson (1911-72)
  Movin' On Up

INDIA

India is a geographical term. It is no
more a united nation than the
Equator.
- Sir Winston Churchill
  (1874-1965)
  Speech, Royal Albert Hall,

London,
18 March 1931

INDIGNATION

Indignation does no good unless it is
backed with a club of sufficient size
to awe the opposition.
- Edgar Watson Howe (1853-1937)
  Ventures in Common Sense

INDISPENSABILITY

There is no indispensable man.
- Franklin Delano Roosevelt
  (1882-1945)
  Campaign speech, New York,
  3 November 1932

INDIVIDUALITY

In proportion to the development of
his individuality, each person
becomes more valuable to himself,
and is therefore capable of being
more valuable to others.
- John Stuart Mill (1806-73)
  On Liberty

INDUSTRY

Life without industry is guilt,
industry without art is brutality.
- John Ruskin (1819-1900)
  *Lectures on Art: The Relation of
  Art to Morals*

INFANTS

No animal is so inexhaustible as an
excited infant.

– Amy Leslie (1860-1939)
  Amy Leslie at the Fair

INFERIORITY

No one can make you feel inferior
without your consent.
– Eleanor Roosevelt (1884-1962)
  This is My Story

INFLATION

Nothing so weakens government as
persistent inflation.
– John Kenneth Galbraith
  (1908-)
  The Affluent Society

I would liken inflation to a cancerous
growth in the economy and society.
When a victim of cancer goes to a
doctor for surgery, the surgeon does
not simply cut out a little of the
growth, because he knows it would
then grow still larger and more lethal
later on. Not gradually but
immediately, a good doctor tries to
cut out all the malignancy. If we
want to stop inflation, we have
likewise to do so by shock treatment:
basically overnight. Ending inflation
inevitably causes transitional
hardship as past expectations adjust
to stable prices. But the longer we
delay, the more severe the surgery
and the necessary readjustment. Let
sceptics ponder the old wisdom:
soonest ended, soonest mended.
– Walter H. Salomon (1906-)
  Speech, Annual General Meeting
  of Rea Brothers Ltd, England,
  19 April 1977

Uncontrolled inflation can lead
progressively to loss of government
credibility, lowering of confidence,
economic stagnation, rising levels of
unemployment, and as a final
consequence to collapse of the
political, economic and social
systems and the drastic and illusory
'cure' of totalitarianism.
– Walter H. Salomon (1906-)
  'How to Cure Inflation and Save
  the Currency', *The Spectator*,
  26 August 1978

Let us repeat and repeat again,
inflation can only be created by
government. Therefore, it can only
be stopped by government.
– Walter H. Salomon (1906-)
  Speech, Annual General Meeting
  of Rea Brothers Ltd, England,
  14 April 1981

INFLUENZA

There was no influenza in my young
days. We called a cold a cold.
– Arnold Bennett (1867-1931)
  The Card

INFORMATION

It is a very sad thing that nowadays
there is so little useless information.
– Oscar Wilde (1854-1900)
  *A Few Maxims for the Instruction
  of the Over-Educated*

INGRATITUDE

Gratitude is the least of Virtues, but
Ingratitude is the worst of Vices.

— Thomas Fuller (1654-1734)
Gnomologia

INJURIES

Neglect kills Injuries, Revenge
increases them.
— Benjamin Franklin (1706-90)
Poor Richard's Almanack, 1749

Women and elephants never forget an
injury.
— Saki (H.H. Munro) (1870-1916)
Reginald, on Besetting Sins

INNOCENCE

Innocence is its own defence.
— Benjamin Franklin (1706-90)
Poor Richard's Almanack, 1733

Innocence is no Protection.
— Thomas Fuller (1654-1734)
Gnomologia

INNOVATIONS

Innovations are dangerous.
— Thomas Fuller (1654-1734)
Gnomologia

INSIGHT

A moment's insight is sometimes
worth a life's experience.
— Oliver Wendell Holmes (1809-94)
*The Professor at the Breakfast-
Table*

INSTRUCTION

Give *instruction* to a wise *man*, and
he will be yet wiser: teach a just *man*,
and he will increase in learning.
— *Bible*, Authorised version
Proverbs, Ch. 9, v. 9

INSULTS

He who allows himself to be insulted,
deserves to be.
— Pierre Corneille (1606-84)
Héraclius

INSURRECTION

Insurrection is an art and like all arts
it has its laws.
— Leon Trotsky (1879-1940)
History of the Russian Revolution

INTELLECTUAL WORLD

The intellectual world is divided into
two classes — dilettantes, on the one
hand, and pedants, on the other.
— Miguel de Unamuno (1864-1936)
The Tragic Sense of Life

INTERPRETER

Interpreter, n. One who enables two
persons of different languages to
understand each other by repeating
to each what it would have been to
the interpreter's advantage for the
other to have said.
— Ambrose Bierce (1842-1914?)
The Devil's Dictionary

INVASION

One can resist the invasion of armies, but not the invasion of ideas.
— Victor Hugo (1802-85)
   Histoire d'un Crime

INVESTMENT

It is very much easier for a rich man to invest and grow richer than for the poor man to begin investing at all.
— Barbara Ward (1914-   )
   The Rich Nations and the Poor Nations

IRISH

In old times people used to try and square the circle; now they try and devise schemes for satisfying the Irish nation.
— Samuel Butler (1835-1902)
   Note Books

IRRESPONSIBILITY

Perhaps it is better to be irresponsible and right than to be responsible and wrong.
— Sir Winston Churchill
   (1874-1965)
   Party Political Broadcast, UK,
   26 August 1950

ITAI DOSHIN

If *itai doshin* (many in body, one in mind) prevails among the people, they will achieve all their goals, whereas in *dotai ishin* (one in body, different in mind), they can achieve nothing remarkable.
— Nichiren Daishonin (1222-82)
   The Major Writings of Nichiren Daishonin: On Itai Doshin

JEALOUSY

Jealousy feeds upon suspicion, and it turns into fury or it ends as soon as we pass from suspicion to certainty.
— Duc de La Rochefoucauld
   (1613-80)
   Maxims

O! beware, my lord, of jealousy;
It is the green-eyed monster which doth mock
The meat it feeds on . . .
— William Shakespeare (1564-1616)
   Othello, Act III, Sc. III

JEWS

Hath not a Jew eyes? hath not a Jew hands, organs, dimensions, senses, affections, passions? fed with the same food, hurt with the same weapons, subject to the same diseases, healed by the same means, warmed and cooled by the same winter and summer, as a Christian is? If you prick us, do we not bleed? if you tickle us, do we not laugh? if you poison us, do we not die? and if you wrong us, shall we not revenge? If we are like you in the rest, we will resemble you in that.
— William Shakespeare (1564-1616)
   The Merchant of Venice, Act III, Sc. I

JOB

job. (A low word now much in use,
of which I cannot tell the etymology.)
(1) A low mean lucrative busy affair.
(2) Petty, piddling work; a piece of
chance work.
- Samuel Johnson (1709-84)
  Dictionary

JOKES

A difference of taste in jokes is a
great strain on the affections.
- George Eliot (1819-80)
  Daniel Deronda

JOURNALISTS

Journalists say a thing that they
know isn't true, in the hope that if
they keep on saying it long enough
it *will* be true.
- Arnold Bennett (1867-1931)
  The Title, Act II

JUDGE

No one should be judge in his own
case.
- Publilius Syrus
  (*c*. 1st century BC)
  Maxims

JUDGEMENT

Everyone complains of his memory,
but no one complains of his
judgement.
- Duc de La Rochefoucauld
  (1613-80)
  Maxims

JUSTICE

The price of justice is eternal
publicity.
- Arnold Bennett (1867-1931)
  Things That Have Interested Me

Justice is my being allowed to do
whatever I like. Injustice is whatever
prevents my doing so.
- Samuel Butler (1835-1902)
  Note Books

Rigid Justice, is the greatest Injustice.
- Thomas Fuller (1654-1734)
  Gnomologia

Justice is a machine that, when
someone has given it a starting push,
rolls on of itself.
- John Galsworthy (1867-1933)
  Justice

For most men the love of justice is
only the fear of suffering injustice.
- Duc de La Rochefoucauld
  (1613-80)
  Maxims

. . . it is universally considered just
that each person should obtain that
(whether good or evil) which he
deserves; and unjust that he should
obtain a good, or be made to undergo
an evil, which he does not deserve.
- John Stuart Mill (1806-73)
  Utilitarianism

We love justice greatly, and just men
but a little.
- Joseph Roux (1834-86)
  Meditations of a Parish Priest

KILLING

One kills a man, one is an assassin;
one kills millions, one is a conqueror;
one kills everybody, one is a god.
– Jean Rostand (1894-1977)
Pensées d'un Biologiste

KINDNESS

No act of kindness, no matter how
small, is ever wasted.
– Aesop (*c.* 550 BC)
The Lion and the Mouse

A forced Kindness deserves no thanks.
– Thomas Fuller (1654-1734)
Gnomologia

Kindness is the noblest Weapon to
conquer with.
– Thomas Fuller
Ibid.

KINGS

Better *is* a poor and a wise child than
an old and foolish king, who will no
more be admonished.
– *Bible*, Authorized version
Ecclesiastes, Ch. 4, v. 13

That the king can do no wrong, is a
necessary and fundamental principle
of the English constitution.
– Sir William Blackstone (1723-80)
*Commentaries on the Laws
of England*

Great though they are, kings are only
human.
– Pierre Corneille (1606-84)
Le Cid

What is a King? – a man condemn'd
to bear
The public burden of the nation's
care.
– Matthew Prior (1664-1721)
Solomon

A King is a thing men have made for
their own sakes, for quietness' sake.
Just as in a family one man is
appointed to buy the meat.
– John Seldon (1584-1654)
Table Talk

All kings is mostly rapscallions.
– Mark Twain (1835-1910)
*The Adventures of Huckleberry
Finn*

KISSES

You should not take a fellow eight
years old
And make him swear to never kiss
the girls.
– Robert Browning (1812-89)
Fra Lippo Lippi

What is a Kisse? Why this, as some
approve;
The sure sweet-Sement, Glue, and
Lime of Love.
– Robert Herrick (1591-1674)
Hesperides: A Kisse

The sound of a kiss is not so loud as
that of a cannon, but its echo lasts a
great deal longer.
– Oliver Wendell Holmes (1809-94)
*The Professor at the Breakfast-
Table*

A legal kiss is never as good as a
stolen one.
– Guy de Maupassant

Kisses / Knowledge

(1850-93)
A Wife's Confession

Kissing don't last: cookery do!
— George Meredith (1828-1909)
  The Ordeal of Richard Feverel

O! a kiss
Long as my exile, sweet as my
  revenge.
— William Shakespeare (1564-1616)
  Coriolanus, Act V, Sc. III

But if a man and a maid care for one
another, does it matter so much if
the maid give the first kiss?
— Alfred, Lord Tennyson (1809-92)
  *The Foresters: Robin Hood and
  Maid Marion*

KNOWLEDGE

They know enough who know how
to learn.
— Henry Brooks Adams
  (1838-1918)
  The Education of Henry Adams

Knowledge itself is power.
— Francis Bacon (1561-1626)
  *Religious Meditations:
  Of Heresies*

He that knew all that ever learning
  writ,
Knew only this — that he knew
  nothing yet.
— Aphra Behn (1640-89)
  The Emperor of the Moon

You never know what is enough
unless you know what is more than
enough.
— William Blake (1757-1827)

*The Marriage of Heaven and Hell:
Proverbs of Hell*

. . . there is a Spanish proverb, which
says very justly, Tell me whom you
live with, and I will tell you who you
are.
— Earl of Chesterfield (1694-1773)
  Letter to his son, 9 October 1747

. . . a man who has great knowledge
from experience and observation, of
the characters, customs, and manners
of mankind, is a being as different
from and as superior to a man of
mere book and systematical
knowledge, as a well-managed horse
is to an ass.
— Earl of Chesterfield (1694-1773)
  Letter to his son, 27 May 1753

We owe almost all our knowledge not
to those who have agreed, but to
those who have differed.
— Reverend C.C. Colton
  (1780?-1832)
  Lacon

There is no knowledge that is not
power.
— Ralph Waldo Emerson (1803-82)
  Society and Solitude: Old Age

Knowledge is the antidote to fear.
— Ralph Waldo Emerson (1803-82)
  Courage

There are three Things extreamly
hard, Steel, a Diamond and to know
one's self.
— Benjamin Franklin (1706-90)
  Poor Richard's Almanack, 1750

Tim was so learned, that he could
name a Horse in nine languages: so
ignorant, that he bought a Cow to

ride on.
— Benjamin Franklin
   Ibid.

Knowledge is power.
— Thomas Hobbes (1588-1679)
   Leviathan

If a little knowledge is dangerous,
where is the man who has so much
as to be out of danger?
— Thomas Henry Huxley (1825-95)
   *On Elemental Instruction in
   Physiology*

Knowledge is of two kinds. We know
a subject ourselves, or we know
where we can find information upon
it.
— Samuel Johnson (1709-84)
   Boswell's Life of Johnson

No man's knowledge here can go
beyond his experience.
— John Locke (1632-1704)
   *Essay Concerning Human
   Understanding*

All genuine knowledge originates in
direct experience.
— Mao Tse-tung (1893-1976)
   On Practice, July, 1937

Bodily exercise, when compulsory,
does no harm to the body; but
knowledge which is acquired under
compulsion obtains no hold on the
mind.
— Plato (*c.* 428-348 BC)
   The Republic

I am never afraid of what I know.
— Anna Sewell (1820-78)
   Black Beauty

Desire of knowledge, like the thirst
of riches, increases ever with the
acquisition of it.
— Laurence Sterne (1713-68)
   Tristram Shandy

LABOUR

Labor is prior to, and independent
of, capital. Capital is only the fruit of
labor, and could never have existed if
labor had not first existed. Labor is
the superior of capital, and deserves
much the higher consideration.
Capital has its rights, which are as
worthy of protection as any other
rights.
— Abraham Lincoln (1809-65)
   First Annual Message to Congress,
   3 December 1861

LANGUAGE

The language most likely to continue
long without alteration, would be
that of a nation raised a little, and
but a little, above barbarity, secluded
from strangers, and totally employed
in procuring the conveniences of life.
— Samuel Johnson (1709-84)
   Dictionary

LAUGHTER

Laughter, n. An interior convulsion,
producing a distortion of the features
and accompanied by inarticulate
noises.
— Ambrose Bierce (1842-1914?)
   The Devil's Dictionary

The most wasted of all our days are
those in which we have not laughed.

Laughter / Law

- Nicolas-Sébastien Chamfort (1741-94)
  Maximes et Pensées

Frequent and loud laughter is the characteristic of folly and ill manners: it is the manner in which the mob express their silly joy at silly things; and they call it being merry. In my mind there is nothing so illiberal, and so ill-bred, as audible laughter.
- Earl of Chesterfield (1694-1773)
  Letter to his son, 9 March 1748

He is not laughed at, that laughs at himself first.
- Thomas Fuller (1654-1734)
  Gnomologia

Laughter is the Hickup of a Fool.
- Thomas Fuller
  Ibid.

Laughter is nothing else but sudden glory arising from some sudden conception of some eminency in ourselves, by comparison with the infirmity of others, or with our own formerly.
- Thomas Hobbes (1588-1679)
  Human Nature

Laughter is by definition healthy.
- Doris Lessing (1919-   )
  The Summer Before the Dark

. . . laugh yourselves into stitches . . .
- William Shakespeare (1564-1616)
  Twelfth Night, Act III, Sc. II

There are few who would not rather be hated than laughed at.
- Sydney Smith (1771-1845)
  Sketches of Moral Philosophy

Laugh and the world laughs with you; Weep, and you weep alone . . .
- Ella Wheeler Wilcox (1855-1919)
  Solitude

LAW

Good laws, if they are not obeyed, do not constitute good government.
- Aristotle (384-322 BC)
  Politics

It usually takes a hundred years to make a law, and then, after it has done its work, it usually takes a hundred years to get rid of it.
- Henry Ward Beecher (1813-87)
  Proverbs from Plymouth Pulpit

Law will never be strong or respected unless it has the sentiment of the people behind it.
- James Bryce (1838-1922)
  The American Commonwealth

Laws are inoperative in war.
- Cicero (106-43 BC)
  Pro Milone

The good of the people is the chief law.
- Cicero (106-43 BC)
  De Legibus

In all governments, there must of necessity be both the law and the sword; laws without arms would give us not liberty, but licentiousness; and arms without laws, would produce not subjection, but slavery. The law, therefore, should be unto the sword what the handle is to the hatchet; it should direct the stroke, and temper the force.
- Reverend C.C. Colton

(1780?-1832)
Lacon

Laws *too gentle* are seldom *obeyed*;
too severe, seldom *executed*.
– Benjamin Franklin (1706-90)
   Poor Richard's Almanack, 1756

The more Laws, the more Offenders.
– Thomas Fuller (1654-1734)
   Gnomologia

Law cannot persuade, where it
cannot punish.
– Thomas Fuller
   Ibid.

Laws grind the poor, and rich men
rule the law.
– Oliver Goldsmith (1728-74)
   The Traveller

Useless laws weaken necessary ones.
– Baron de Montesquieu (1689-1755)
   L'Esprit des Lois

The law must be stable, but it must
not stand still.
– Roscoe Pound (1870-1964)
   *Introduction to the Philosophy
   of Law*

For many persons, law appears to be
black magic – an obscure domain
that can be fathomed only by the
professional initiated into its
mysteries.
– Susan C. Ross (1942-   )
   The Rights of Women

Laws are like cobwebs, which may
catch small flies, but let wasps and
hornets break through.
– Jonathan Swift (1667-1745)
   *A Tritical Essay upon the
   Faculties of the Mind*

LAWYERS

A good Lawyer is a bad Neighbour.
– Benjamin Franklin (1706-90)
   Poor Richard's Almanack, 1737

Fools and obstinate Men make the
Lawyers rich.
– Thomas Fuller (1654-1734)
   Gnomologia

There's no better way of exercising
the imagination than the study of
law. No poet ever interpreted nature
as freely as a lawyer interprets truth.
– Jean Giraudoux (1882-1944)
   Tiger at the Gates

The first thing we do, let's kill all
the lawyers.
– William Shakespeare (1564-1616)
   King Henry VI, Pt. II, Act IV,
   Sc. II

LEADERSHIP

The art of leadership . . . consists in
consolidating the attention of the
people against a single adversary and
taking care that nothing will split up
that attention.
– Adolf Hitler (1889-1945)
   Mein Kampf

It is time for a new generation of
leadership, to cope with new
problems and new opportunities. For
there is a new world to be won.
– John F. Kennedy (1917-63)
   Speech, US television,
   4 July 1960

When the tyrant has disposed of
foreign enemies by conquest or
treaty, and there is nothing to fear

from them, then he is always stirring
up some war or other, in order that
the people may require a leader.
- Plato (*c.* 428-348 BC)
  The Republic

LEARNING

Learning is not attained by chance,
it must be sought for with ardor and
attended to with diligence.
- Abigail Adams (1744-1818)
  Letter to John Quincy Adams,
  8 May 1780

It is always the season for the old
to learn.
- Aeschylus (525-456 BC)
  Fragments

What we have to learn to do, we learn
by doing.
- Aristotle (384-322 BC)
  Nicomachean Ethics

Learning without thought is labour
lost; thought without learning is
perilous.
- Confucius (551-479 BC)
  Analects

Wise Men learn by others harms;
Fools by their own.
- Benjamin Franklin (1706-90)
  Poor Richard's Almanack, 1749

There is much more Learning than
Knowledge in the World.
- Thomas Fuller (1654-1734)
  Gnomologia

LECTURERS

All lecturers, all professors, all
schoolmasters, have ruts and grooves
in their minds into which their
conversation is perpetually sliding.
- Oliver Wendell Holmes (1809-94)
  *The Autocrat of the Breakfast-
  Table*

LECTURES

A lecture ought to be something
which all can understand, about
something which interests everybody.
- Oliver Wendell Holmes (1809-94)
  *The Autocrat of the Breakfast-
  Table*

LEISURE

Leisure is the mother of Philosophy.
- Thomas Hobbes (1588-1679)
  Leviathan

LENDING

Lend Money to an Enemy, and
thou'lt gain him, to a Friend and
thou'lt lose him.
- Benjamin Franklin (1706-90)
  Poor Richard's Almanack, 1740

A ready Way to lose your Friend, is
to lend him Money.
- Thomas Fuller (1654-1734)
  Gnomologia

LETTERS

I have received no more than one or
two letters in my life that were worth

the postage.
– Henry David Thoreau (1817-62)
  Walden

LEXICOGRAPHER

Lexicographer, n. A pestilent fellow
who, under the pretense of recording
some particular stage in the
development of a language, does
what he can to arrest its growth,
stiffen its flexibility and mechanize
its methods.
– Ambrose Bierce (1842-1914?)
  The Devil's Dictionary

lexicographer. A writer of
dictionaries; a harmless drudge, that
busies himself in tracing the original,
and detailing the signification of
words.
– Samuel Johnson (1709-84)
  Dictionary

LIARS

Liars ought to have good memories.
– Algernon Sidney (1622-83)
  *Discourses Concerning
  Government*

If you want to be thought a liar,
always tell the truth.
– Logan Pearsall Smith (1865-1946)
  Afterthoughts

LIBERALISM

The essence of the Liberal outlook
lies not in *what* opinions are held,
but in *how* they are held: instead of
being held dogmatically, they are
held tentatively, and with a

consciousness that new evidence may
at any moment lead to their
abandonment.
– Bertrand Russell (1872-1970)
  *Unpopular Essays: Philosophy
  and Politics*

LIBERTY

A day, an hour of virtuous liberty
Is worth a whole eternity in bondage.
– Joseph Addison (1672-1719)
  Cato, Act II

. . . proclaim liberty throughout *all*
the land unto all the inhabitants
thereof.
– *Bible*, Authorized version
  Leviticus, Ch. 25, v. 10

Liberty, n. One of Imagination's
most precious possessions.
– Ambrose Bierce (1842-1914?)
  The Devil's Dictionary

Lean Liberty is better than fat
Slavery.
– Thomas Fuller (1654-1734)
  Gnomologia

The liberty of the press is most
generally approved when it takes
liberties with the other fellow, and
leaves us alone.
– Edgar Watson Howe (1853-1937)
  Country Town Sayings

The tree of liberty must be refreshed
from time to time with the blood of
patriots and tyrants. It is its natural
manure.
– Thomas Jefferson (1743-1826)
  Letter to W.S. Smith,
  13 November 1787

Liberty / Life

... the sole end for which mankind are warranted, individually or collectively, in interfering with the liberty of action of any of their number, is self-protection. That the only purpose for which power can be rightfully exercised over any member of a civilised community, against his will, is to prevent harm to others. His own good, either physical or moral, is not a sufficient warrant.
– John Stuart Mill (1806-73)
  On Liberty

The liberty of the individual must be thus far limited; he must not make himself a nuisance to other people.
– John Stuart Mill
  Ibid.

Liberty means responsibility. That is why most men dread it.
– George Bernard Shaw
  (1856-1950)
  Man and Superman: Maxims for Revolutionists

LIES

There are three kinds of lies: lies, damned lies, and statistics.
– Mark Twain (1835-1910)
  Autobiography

LIFE

... I am one of those people who just can't help getting a kick out of life – even when it's a kick in the teeth.
– Polly Adler (1900-62)
  A House is Not a Home

The quality of a life is determined by its activities.
– Aristotle (384-322 BC)
  Nicomachean Ethics

The life of every man is a diary in which he means to write one story, and writes another; and his humblest hour is when he compares the volume as it is with what he vowed to make it.
– J.M. Barrie (1860-1937)
  The Little Minister

Life is rather like a tin of sardines – we're all of us looking for the key.
– Alan Bennett (1934-   )
  Beyond the Fringe

Life is one long process of getting tired.
– Samuel Butler (1835-1902)
  Note Books

Life is the art of drawing sufficient conclusions from insufficient premises.
– Samuel Butler
  Ibid.

Is life worth living? This is a question for an embryo not for a man.
– Samuel Butler
  Ibid.

Life's too short for chess.
– H.J. Byron (1834-84)
  Our Boys, Act I

When you look into your own mind at any moment, you perceive neither colour nor form to verify that it exists. Yet you still cannot say it does not exist, for many differing thoughts continually occur to you. Life is indeed an elusive reality that

transcends both the words and
concepts of existence and nonexistence. It is neither existence nor
nonexistence, yet exhibits the
qualities of both.
– Nichiren Daishonin (1222-82)
  *The Major Writings of Nichiren
  Daishonin: On Attaining
  Buddahood*

I have measured out my life with
coffee spoons.
– T.S. Eliot (1888-1965)
  *The Love Song of J. Alfred
  Prufrock*

Life never gives us what we want at
the moment that we consider
appropriate.
– E.M. Forster (1879-1970)
  A Passage to India

To lengthen thy Life, lessen thy
Meals.
– Benjamin Franklin (1706-90)
  Poor Richard's Almanack, 1733

Life is half spent, before we know
what it is.
– Thomas Fuller (1654-1734)
  Gnomologia

The longest Life is but a Parcel of
Moments.
– Thomas Fuller
  Ibid.

Life is a jest; and all things show it.
I thought so once; but now I know it.
– John Gay (1685-1732)
  My Own Epitaph

Life's a pudding full of plums.
– W.S. Gilbert (1836-1911)
  The Gondoliers

Life is made up of sobs, sniffles, and
smiles, with sniffles predominating.
– O. Henry (1862-1910)
  The Gift of the Magi

Life is a series of compromises.
– Cyrus Hepplewaite (1807-1900)
  The Way to Live

I always believed in life rather than
in books.
– Oliver Wendell Holmes (1809-94)
  *The Autocrat of the Breakfast-
  Table*

Life is just one damned thing after
another.
– Elbert Hubbard (1856-1915)
  A Thousand and One Epigrams

Life isn't all beer and skittles.
– Thomas Hughes (1822-96)
  Tom Brown's Schooldays

It matters not how a man dies but
how he lives.
– Samuel Johnson (1709-84)
  Boswell's Life of Johnson

Life is a progress from want to want,
not from enjoyment to enjoyment.
– Samuel Johnson
  Ibid.

I compare human life to a large
mansion of many apartments, two of
which I can only describe, the doors
of the rest being as yet shut upon me.
– John Keats (1795-1821)
  Letter to John Hamilton
  Reynolds, 3 May 1818

Life is either a daring adventure or
nothing.
– Helen Keller (1880-1968)
  Let Us Have Faith

Life / Literature

Life can only be understood backwards; but it must be lived forwards.
– Sören Kierkegaard (1813-55)
Life

Life is a crooked Labyrinth . . .
– Henry King (1592-1669)
The Labyrinth

What is life but a series of preludes to that unknown song whose first solemn note is sounded by death?
– Alphonse de Lamartine (1790-1869)
Méditations Poétiques

Life is real! Life is earnest!
And the grave is not its goal . . .
– Henry Wadsworth Longfellow (1807-82)
A Psalm of Life

Life is one long struggle in the dark.
– Lucretius (*c*. 94-55 BC)
De Rerum Natura

Our lives are rivers whose outlet is the sea of death.
– Jorge Manrique (1440-79)
Coplas por la Muerte de su Padre

He who lets the world, or his own portion of it, choose his plan of life for him, has no need of any other faculty than the ape-like one of imitation.
– John Stuart Mill (1806-73)
On Liberty

One crowded hour of glorious life
Is worth an age without a name.
– Sir Walter Scott (1771-1832)
Old Mortality

Life is as tedious as a twice-told tale,
Vexing the dull ear of a drowsy man.
– William Shakespeare (1564-1616)
King John, Act III, Sc. IV

Live as long as you may, the first twenty years are the longest half of your life.
– Robert Southey (1774-1843)
The Doctor

Life is a tragedy wherein we sit as spectators for a while and then act our part in it.
– Jonathan Swift (1667-1745)
Thoughts on Various Subjects

The mass of men lead lives of quiet desperation.
– Henry David Thoreau (1817-62)
Walden

I thought life was going to be a brilliant comedy . . .
– Oscar Wilde (1854-1900)
De Profundis

LITERATURE

Literature is the art of writing something that will be read twice; journalism what will be grasped at once.
– Cyril Connolly (1903-74)
Enemies of Promise

He knew everything about literature except how to enjoy it.
– Joseph Heller (1923-   )
Catch-22

That was the chief difference between literature and life. In books, the proportion of exceptional to commonplace people is high; in

reality, very low.
— Aldous Huxley (1894-1963)
  Eyeless in Gaza

Literature flourishes best when it is
half a trade and half an art.
— Dean Inge (1860-1954)
  The Victorian Age

But what is the difference between
literature and journalism? . . .
journalism is unreadable, and
literature is not read.
— Oscar Wilde (1854-1900)
  The Critic as Artist

LONDON

Oh, London is a fine town,
A very famous city,
Where all the streets are paved with
  gold,
And all the maidens pretty.
— George Colman (the Younger)
  (1762-1836)
  The Heir-at-Law

London, the great cesspool into
which all the loungers of the Empire
are irresistibly drained.
— Sir Arthur Conan Doyle
  (1859-1930)
  A Study in Scarlet

. . . when a man is tired of London he
is tired of life; for there is in London
all that life can afford.
— Samuel Johnson (1709-84)
  Boswell's Life of Johnson

LOVE

Love is, above all, the gift of
oneself.

— Jean Anouilh (1910-   )
  Ardèle

Let no one who loves be called
altogether unhappy. Even love
unreturned has its rainbow.
— J.M. Barrie (1860-1937)
  The Little Minister

Greater love hath no man than this,
that a man lay down his life for his
friends.
— *Bible*, Authorized version
  St John, Ch. 15, v. 13

Better *is* a dinner of herbs where love
is, than a stalled ox and hatred
therewith.
— *Bible*, Authorized version
  Proverbs, Ch. 15, v. 17

I prize thy love more than whole
Mines of gold.
— Anne Bradstreet (1612-72)
  To My Dear And Loving Husband

Alas! the love of women! it is known
To be a lovely and a fearful thing.
— Lord Byron (1788-1824)
  Don Juan

Man's love is of man's life a thing
  apart,
'Tis woman's whole existence.
— Lord Byron
  Ibid.

In her first passion woman loves
  her lover,
In all the others all she loves is love.
— Lord Byron
  Ibid.

Love in young men, for the most
part, is not love but simply sexual
desire and its accomplishment is its

Love

end.
- Miguel de Cervantes (1547-1616)
  Don Quixote

Love, in the form in which it exists in society, is nothing but the exchange of two fantasies and the contact of two bodies.
- Nicolas-Sébastien Chamfort (1741-94)
  Maximes et Pensées

Love is blynd.
- Geoffrey Chaucer (1340?-1400)
  The Canterbury Tales: The Merchant's Tale

Ideal love is a lie put forth by poets.
- Alphonse Daudet (1840-97)
  Tartarin sur les Alpes

Love built on beauty, soone as beauty, dies.
- John Donne (1572-1631)
  The Anagram

Give all to love;
Obey thy heart.
- Ralph Waldo Emerson (1803-82)
  Give All To Love

Love and scandal are the best sweeteners of tea.
- Henry Fielding (1707-54)
  Love in Several Masques

What is commonly called love, namely the desire of satisfying a voracious appetite with a certain quantity of delicate white human flesh.
- Henry Fielding (1707-54)
  Tom Jones

He that falls in love with himself, will have no Rivals.

- Benjamin Franklin (1706-90)
  Poor Richard's Almanack, 1739

If you would be loved, love and be loveable.
- Benjamin Franklin
  Ibid., 1755

If you love yourself too much, nobody else will love you at all.
- Thomas Fuller (1654-1734)
  Gnomologia

She who has never lov'd, has never liv'd.
- John Gay (1685-1732)
  The Captives, Act II

It's love that makes the world go round.
- W.S. Gilbert (1836-1911)
  Iolanthe

Love is that condition in which the happiness of another person is essential to your own.
- Robert A. Heinlein (1907-   )
  Stranger in a Strange Land

Love is like the measles; we all have to go through it.
- Jerome K. Jerome (1859-1927)
  The Idle Thoughts of an Idle Fellow

Love's like the measles — all the worse when it comes late in life.
- Douglas Jerrold (1803-57)
  Wit and Opinions of Douglas Jerrold

I equally dislike the favour of the public with the love of a woman — they are both a cloying treacle to the wings of independence.
- John Keats (1795-1821)

Letter to John Taylor,
24 August 1819

She look'd at me as she did love,
And made sweet moan.
– John Keats (1795-1821)
  La Belle Dame Sans Merci

Love like ours can never die!
– Rudyard Kipling (1865-1936)
  The Lovers' Litany

True love is like a psychic experience.
Everyone tells ghost stories, but few
have ever seen a ghost.
– Duc de La Rochefoucauld
  (1613-80)
  Maxims

Where both deliberate, the love is
  slight;
Who ever lov'd, that lov'd not at first
  sight?
– Christopher Marlowe (1564-93)
  Hero and Leander

Love is the business of the idle, but
the idleness of the busy.
– Owen Meredith (Edward Robert
  Bulwer-Lytton, Earl of Lytton),
  (1831-91)
  Rienzi

A woman has got to love a bad man
once or twice in her life, to be
thankful for a good one.
– Marjorie Kinnan Rawlings
  (1896-1953)
  The Yearling

I love you more than yesterday, less
than tomorrow.
– Edmond Rostand (1868-1918)
  Les Musardises

Love is something far more than
desire for sexual intercourse; it is
the principal means of escape from
the loneliness which afflicts most
men and women throughout the
greater part of their lives.
– Bertrand Russell (1872-1970)
  Marriage and Morals

To fear love is to fear life, and those
who fear life are already three parts
dead.
– Bertrand Russell
  Ibid.

True love's the gift which God has
  given
To man alone beneath the heaven.
– Sir Walter Scott (1771-1832)
  The Lay of the Last Minstrel

The course of true love never did
run smooth . . .
– William Shakespeare (1564-1616)
  A Midsummer-Night's Dream;
  Act I, Sc. I

If thou remember'st not the slightest
  folly
That ever love did make thee run
  into,
Thou hast not loved.
– William Shakespeare (1564-1616)
  As You Like It, Act II, Sc. IV

Love is merely a madness . . .
– William Shakespeare
  Ibid., Act III, Sc. II

Love comforteth like sunshine after
  rain,
But Lust's effect is tempest after sun;
Love's gentle spring doth always
  fresh remain,
Lust's winter comes ere summer half
  be done.

Love / Lying

Love surfeits not, Lust like a
  glutton dies;
Love is all truth, Lust full of
  forged lies.
— William Shakespeare (1564-1616)
  Venus and Adonis

Love sought is good, but given
unsought is better.
— William Shakespeare (1564-1616)
  Twelfth Night, Act III, Sc. I

Love is the whole history of a
woman's life, it is but an episode in a
man's.
— Madame de Staël (1766-1817)
  De l'Influence des Passions

In the Spring a young man's fancy
lightly turns to thoughts of love.
— Alfred, Lord Tennyson (1809-92)
  Locksley Hall

'Tis better to have loved and lost
Than never to have loved at all.
— Alfred, Lord Tennyson (1809-92)
  In Memoriam

Some cynical Frenchman has said
that there are two parties to a love
transaction: the one who loves and
the other who condescends to be so
treated.
— William Makepeace Thackeray
  (1811-63)
  Vanity Fair

Love is like any other luxury. You
have no right to it unless you can
afford it.
— Anthony Trollope (1815-82)
  The Way We Live Now

We always believe our first love is our
last, and our last love our first.
— George Whyte-Melville

(1821-78)
Katerfelto

I see when men love women
They give them but a little of their
  lives
But women when they love give
  everything.
— Oscar Wilde (1854-1900)
  The Duchess of Padua, Act III

LOVERS

It is easier to be a lover than a
husband for the simple reason that it
is more difficult to be witty every
day than to say pretty things from
time to time.
— Honoré de Balzac (1799-1850)
  Physiologie du Mariage

Lovers never get tired of each other,
because they are always talking about
themselves.
— Duc de La Rochefoucauld
  (1613-80)
  Maxims

We that are true lovers run into
strange capers . . .
— William Shakespeare (1564-1616)
  As You Like It, Act II, Sc. IV

LYING

I do not mind lying, but I hate
inaccuracy.
— Samuel Butler (1835-1902)
  Note Books

Lying has a kind of respect and
reverence with it. We pay a person
the compliment of acknowledging his
superiority whenever we lie to him.

– Samuel Butler
Ibid.

Any fool can tell the truth, but it requires a man of some sense to know how to lie well.
– Samuel Butler
Ibid.

He who permits himself to tell a lie once, finds it much easier to do it a second and third time, till at length it becomes habitual . . .
– Thomas Jefferson (1743-1826)
Letter to Peter Carr,
19 August 1785

Let me have no lying; it becomes none but tradesmen . . .
– William Shakespeare (1564-1616)
The Winter's Tale, Act IV, Sc. IV

Lord, Lord! how subject we old men are to this vice of lying.
– William Shakespeare (1564-1616)
King Henry IV, Pt. II, Act III,
Sc. II

MACHINES

One machine can do the work of fifty ordinary men. No machine can do the work of one extraordinary man.
– Elbert Hubbard (1856-1915)
The Philistines

MAN

Man is by nature a political animal.
– Aristotle (384-322 BC)
Politics

And the LORD God formed man *of* the dust of the ground, and breathed into his nostrils the breath of life; and man became a living soul.
– *Bible*, Authorized version
Genesis, Ch. 2, v. 7

Man is the only animal that can remain on friendly terms with the victims he intends to eat until he eats them.
– Samuel Butler (1835-1902)
Note Books

Man is God's highest present development. He is the latest thing in God.
– Samuel Butler
Ibid.

Man is a tool-using animal. Without tools he is nothing, with tools he is all.
– Thomas Carlyle (1795-1881)
Sartor Resartus

Man is an embodied paradox, a bundle of contradictions.
– Reverend C.C. Colton
(1780?-1832)
Lacon

Man is a pliable animal, a being who gets accustomed to everything.
– Feodor Mikhailovich Dostoevsky
(1821-81)
The House of the Dead

Man is the only animal that laughs and weeps; for he is the only animal that is struck with the difference between what things are, and what they ought to be.
– William Hazlitt (1778-1830)
Lectures on the English Comic Writers

In the study of Man it is easier to understand the species than the individual.
- Duc de La Rochefoucauld (1613-80)
  Maxims

Man, I can assure you, is a nasty animal.
- Molière (1622-73)
  Le Tartuffe, Act V

The proper study of Mankind is Man.
- Alexander Pope (1688-1744)
  An Essay on Man

Man is a reasoning animal.
- Seneca (*c.* 4 BC-65 AD)
  Epistles

There are many wonderful things in nature, but the most wonderful of all is man.
- Sophocles (*c.* 495-406 BC)
  Antigone

Man is a social animal.
- Benedict Spinoza (1632-77)
  Ethics

Man is the hunter; woman is his game.
- Alfred, Lord Tennyson (1809-92)
  The Princess: A Medley

MANNERS

Fine manners need the support of fine manners in others.
- Ralph Waldo Emerson (1803-82)
  The Conduct of Life

MARRIAGE

Happiness in marriage is entirely a matter of chance.
- Jane Austen (1775-1817)
  Pride and Prejudice

It is a truth universally acknowledged, that a single man in possession of a good fortune, must be in want of a wife.
- Jane Austen
  Ibid.

Women — one half the human race at least — care fifty times more for a marriage than a ministry.
- Walter Bagehot (1826-77)
  The English Constitution

Marriage always demands the greatest understanding of the art of insincerity possible between two human beings.
- Vicki Baum (1888-1960)
  And Life Goes On

Well-married, a man is winged — ill-matched, he is shackled.
- Henry Ward Beecher (1813-87)
  Proverbs from Plymouth Pulpit

. . . it is better to marry than to burn.
- *Bible*, Authorized version
  1 *Corinthians*, Ch. 7, v. 9

One was never married, and that's his hell; another is, and that's his plague.
- Robert Burton (1577-1640)
  Anatomy of Melancholy

They say it is so selfish of men not to marry: perhaps it is; but is it not selfish of women to insist on men marrying them?

– Samuel Butler (1835-1902)
Note Books

Though women are angels, yet
wedlock's the devil.
– Lord Byron (1788-1824)
Hours of Idleness: To Eliza

Though marriage makes man and
wife one flesh, it leaves 'em still two
fools.
– William Congreve (1670-1729)
The Double Dealer, Act II

Every woman should marry – and
no man.
– Benjamin Disraeli (1804-81)
Lothair

Any intelligent woman who reads the
marriage contract, and then goes
into it, deserves all the consequences.
– Isadora Duncan (1878-1927)
My Life

The joys of marriage are the heaven
on earth.
– John Ford (*c.* 1586-1639)
The Broken Heart, Act II

Ne'er take a wife till thou hast a
house (and a fire) to put her in.
– Benjamin Franklin (1706-90)
Poor Richard's Almanack, 1733

Keep your eyes wide open before
marriage, half shut afterwards.
– Benjamin Franklin
Ibid., 1738

He that marrieth for Wealth, sells his
Liberty.
– Thomas Fuller (1654-1734)
Gnomologia

Who marrieth for Love without
Money, hath merry Night and sorry
Days.
– Thomas Fuller
Ibid.

If Marriages are made in Heaven, you
had few Friends there.
– Thomas Fuller
Ibid.

The fundamental error of their
matrimonial union; that of having
based a permanent contract on a
temporary feeling.
– Thomas Hardy (1840-1928)
Jude the Obscure

If men knew how women pass the
time when they are alone, they'd
never marry.
– O. Henry (1862-1910)
Memoirs of a Yellow Dog

The critical period in matrimony is
breakfast-time.
– A.P. Herbert (1890-1971)
Uncommon Law

Marriage is a good deal like a circus:
there is not as much in it as is
represented in the advertising.
– Edgar Watson Howe (1853-1937)
Country Town Sayings

Marriage has many pains, but
celibacy has no pleasures.
– Samuel Johnson (1709-84)
Rasselas

There is no more lovely, friendly and
charming relationship, communion or
company than a good marriage.
– Martin Luther (1483-1546)
Table Talk

Marriage

Better to be married than dead!
— Molière (1622-73)
  Les Fourberies de Scapin

Marrying a stupid woman will
prevent you from looking stupid.
— Molière (1622-73)
  L'Ecole des Femmes

Marriage is like a cage; one sees the
birds outside desperate to get in, and
those inside equally desperate to get
out.
— Michel Eyquem de Montaigne
  (1533-92)
  Essays

Marriage is a covenant which hath
nothing free but the entrance.
— Michel Eyquem de Montaigne
  Ibid.

Saw a wedding in the church; and
strange to see what delight we
married people have to see these poor
fools decoyed into our condition.
— Samuel Pepys (1633-1703)
  Diary, 25 December 1665

When you see what some girls marry,
you realize how they must hate to
work for a living.
— Helen Rowland (1876-1950)
  Reflections of a Bachelor Girl

Marriage is the ultimate goal of love.
— George Sand (1804-76)
  Story of My Life

To marry is to halve your rights and
double your duties.
— Arthur Schopenhauer
  (1788-1860)
  The World as Will and Idea

Marriage is a desperate thing.
— John Selden (1584-1654)
  Table Talk

A young man married is a man that's
marr'd.
— William Shakespeare (1564-1616)
  All's Well That Ends Well, Act II,
  Sc. III

Marriage is popular because it
combines the maximum of
temptation with the maximum of
opportunity.
— George Bernard Shaw
  (1856-1950)
  *Man and Superman: Maxims
  for Revolutionists*

It is a woman's business to get
married as soon as possible, and a
man's to keep unmarried as long as
he can.
— George Bernard Shaw
  (1856-1950)
  Man and Superman, Act II

Marriage resembles a pair of shears,
so joined that they can not be
separated; often moving in opposite
directions; yet always punishing
anyone who comes between them.
— Sydney Smith (1771-1845)
  *A Memoir of the Reverend
  Sydney Smith* by Lady Holland

In marriage, a man becomes slack and
selfish, and undergoes a fatty
degeneration of his moral being.
— Robert Louis Stevenson
  (1850-94)
  Virginibus Puerisque

Times are changed with him who
marries; there are no more by-path
meadows, where you may innocently

linger, but the road lies long and straight and dusty to the grave.
- Robert Louis Stevenson
  Ibid.

The reason why so few marriages are happy, is, because young ladies spend their time in making nets, not in making cages.
- Jonathan Swift (1667-1745)
  Thoughts on Various Subjects

Marriage is the only adventure open to the timid.
- Voltaire (1694-1778)
  Pensées d'un Philosophe

Twenty years of romance makes a woman look like a ruin; but twenty years of marriage make her something like a public building.
- Oscar Wilde (1854-1900)
  A Woman of No Importance,
  Act I

All the unhappy marriages come from the husbands having brains. What good are brains to a man? They only unsettle him.
- P.G. Wodehouse (1881-1975)
  The Adventures of Sally

MASSES

All the world over, I will back the masses against the classes.
- William Gladstone (1809-98)
  Speech, Liverpool, England,
  28 June 1886

The Masses are more Knowing and more Constant than is a Prince.
- Niccolo Machiavelli (1469-1527)
  Discourses

MATHEMATICS

Mathematics, rightly viewed, possesses not only truth, but supreme beauty – a beauty cold and austere, like that of sculpture, without appeal to any part of our weaker nature, without the gorgeous trappings of painting or music, yet sublimely pure, and capable of a stern perfection such as only the greatest art can show.
- Bertrand Russell (1872-1970)
  The Study of Mathematics

MAY

A windy March and a rainy April, make a beautiful May.
- Thomas Fuller (1654-1734)
  Gnomologia

MEALS

Unquiet meals make ill digestions.
- William Shakespeare (1564-1616)
  The Comedy of Errors, Act V,
  Sc. I

MEDICINE

I find the medicine worse than the malady.
- Francis Beaumont (1584-1616)
  and John Fletcher (1579-1625)
  The Lovers' Progress, Act III

MEDIOCRITY

Mediocrity knows nothing higher than itself, but talent instantly recognizes genius.

Mediocrity / Mercy

- Sir Arthur Conan Doyle
  (1859-1930)
  The Valley of Fear

In sober truth, whatever homage may
be professed, or even paid, to real or
supposed mental superiority, the
general tendency of things
throughout the world is to render
mediocrity the ascendant power
among mankind.
- John Stuart Mill (1806-73)
  On Liberty

MEEKNESS

Meekness, n. Uncommon patience in
planning a revenge that is worth
while.
- Ambrose Bierce (1842-1914?)
  The Devil's Dictionary

Meekness is the mask of malice.
- Robert G. Ingersoll (1833-99)
  Prose-Poems and Selections

MEGALOMANIACS

The megalomaniac differs from the
narcissist by the fact that he wishes
to be powerful rather than charming,
and seeks to be feared rather than
loved. To this type belong many
lunatics and most of the great men of
history.
- Bertrand Russell (1872-1970)
  The Conquest of Happiness

MEMORIES

Memories are hunting horns whose
sound dies on the wind.
- Guillaume Apollinaire

(1880-1918)
Cors de Chasse

MEMORY

It is notorious that the memory
strengthens as you lay burdens upon
it, and becomes trustworthy as you
trust it.
- Thomas de Quincey (1785-1859)
  *Confessions of an English
  Opium-Eater*

Many complain of their Memory, few
of their Judgment.
- Benjamin Franklin (1706-90)
  Poor Richard's Almanack, 1745

MEN

Men are what their mothers made
them.
- Ralph Waldo Emerson (1803-82)
  The Conduct of Life

. . . men of few words are the best
men . . .
- William Shakespeare (1564-1616)
  King Henry V, Act III, Sc. II

MERCENARIES

. . . with mercenaries your greatest
danger is from their cowardice . . .
- Niccolo Machiavelli (1469-1527)
  The Prince

MERCY

Ultimately, mercy is the surest sign
by which the world may distinguish a
true king.

— Pierre Corneille (1606-84)
Cinna

MERIT

Money cannot buy Merit.
— Thomas Fuller (1654-1734)
Gnomologia

METAPHYSICS

Metaphysics is the finding of bad
reasons for what we believe upon
instinct.
— F.H. Bradley (1846-1924)
Appearance and Reality

Metaphysics is the attempt of the
mind to rise above the mind.
— Thomas Carlyle (1795-1881)
Characteristics

METHODS

You know my method. It is founded
upon the observance of trifles.
— Sir Arthur Conan Doyle
(1859-1930)
The Boscombe Valley Mystery

MIDDLE WAY

I agree with you that in politics the
middle way is none at all.
— John Adams (1735-1826)
Letter to Horatio Gates,
23 March 1776

MILITARY

The professional military mind is
by necessity an inferior and
unimaginative mind; no man of high
intellectual quality would willingly
imprison his gifts in such a calling.
— H.G. Wells (1866-1946)
The Outline of History

MIND

It is not enough to have a good mind.
The main thing is to use it well.
— René Descartes (1596-1650)
Le Discours de la Méthode

MINISTERS

An upright minister asks, *what*
recommends a man; a corrupt
minister *who*.
— Reverend C.C. Colton
(1780?-1832)
Lacon

MINORITY

The minority is always right.
— Henrik Ibsen (1828-1906)
An Enemy of the People, Act IV

MISERY

It is a miserable state of mind to have
few things to desire and many things
to fear.
— Francis Bacon (1561-1626)
Essays: Of Empire

Misery loves company.
— John Ray

Misery / Moderation

(1627-1705)
English Proverbs

. . . misery acquaints a man with
strange bed-fellows.
— William Shakespeare (1564-1616)
The Tempest, Act II, Sc. II

MISFORTUNES

I am convinced that we have a degree
of delight, and that no small one, in
the real misfortunes and pains of
others.
— Edmund Burke (1729-97)
On the Sublime and Beautiful

We are all strong enough to endure
the misfortunes of others.
— Duc de La Rochefoucauld
(1613-80)
Maxims

The world is quickly bored by the
recital of misfortune, and willingly
avoids the sight of distress.
— Somerset Maugham (1874-1965)
The Moon and Sixpence

MISQUOTE

With just enough of learning to
misquote.
— Lord Byron (1788-1824)
*English Bards and Scotch
Reviewers*

MISTAKES

The man who makes no mistakes
does not usually make anything.
— Edward John Phelps (1822-1900)
Speech at the Mansion House,

London, on
24 January 1899

We often discover what *will* do, by
finding out what will not do; and
probably he who never made a
mistake never made a discovery.
— Samuel Smiles (1812-1904)
Self-Help

MISTRESSES

Eighth and lastly. They are so
grateful!!
— Benjamin Franklin (1706-90)
*Reasons for Preferring an Elderly
Mistress*

A mistress should be like a little
country retreat near the town, not to
dwell in constantly, but only for a
night and away.
— William Wycherley (1640?-1716)
The Country Wife, Act I

MODERATION

Be temperate in wine, in eating,
girls & sloth;
Or the Gout will seize you and plague
you both.
— Benjamin Franklin (1706-90)
Poor Richard's Almanack, 1734

Moderation is the silken string
running through the pearl chain of all
virtues.
— Joseph Hall (Bishop of Norwich)
(1574-1656)
Christian Moderation

MODESTY

He who speaks without modesty will find it difficult to make his words good.
— Confucius (551- 479 BC)
Analects

Great Modesty often hides great Merit.
— Benjamin Franklin (1706-90)
Poor Richard's Almanack, 1758

Even if we achieve gigantic successes in our work, there is no reason whatsoever to feel conceited and arrogant. Modesty helps one to go forward, whereas conceit makes one lag behind. This is a truth we must always bear in mind.
— Mao Tse-tung (1893-1976)
Opening Address, Eighth National Congress of the Communist Party of China, 15 September 1956

MOMENTS

Our latest moment is always our supreme moment. Five minutes delay in dinner now is more important than a great sorrow ten years gone.
— Samuel Butler (1835-1902)
Note Books

MONARCHY

The best reason why Monarchy is a strong government is, that it is an intelligible government. The mass of mankind understand it, and they hardly anywhere in the world understand any other.
— Walter Bagehot (1826-77)
The English Constitution

The greatest monarch on the proudest throne, is oblig'd to sit upon his own arse.
— Benjamin Franklin (1706-90)
Poor Richard's Almanack, 1737

MONEY

Money is like muck, not good except it be spread.
— Francis Bacon (1561-1626)
Essays: Of Seditions and Troubles

Money speaks sense in a language all nations understand.
— Aphra Behn (1640-89)
The Rover, Pt. II, Act III

It has been said that the love of money is the root of all evil. The want of money is so quite as truly.
— Samuel Butler (1835-1902)
Erewhon

The sinews of art and literature like those of war, are money.
— Samuel Butler (1835-1902)
Note Books

Next to sexual matters there are none upon which there is such complete reserve between parents and children as on those connected with money.
— Samuel Butler
Ibid.

Money is the last enemy that shall ever be subdued. While there is flesh there is money — or the want of money, but money is always on the brain so long as there is a brain in reasonable order.
— Samuel Butler
Ibid.

Money

Money, which represents the prose of life, and which is hardly spoken of in parlours without an apology, is, in its effects and laws, as beautiful as roses.
– Ralph Waldo Emerson (1803-82)
  Essays: Nominalist and Realist

Among mankind money is far more persuasive than logical argument.
– Euripides (*c.* 485-406 BC)
  Medea

He that is of Opinion Money will do every Thing, may well be suspected of doing every Thing for Money.
– Benjamin Franklin (1706-90)
  Poor Richard's Almanack, 1753

Love does much; but Money does more.
– Thomas Fuller (1654-1734)
  Gnomologia

Money makes not so many true Friends as real Enemies.
– Thomas Fuller
  Ibid.

Money, like Dung, does no Good till 'tis spread.
– Thomas Fuller
  Ibid.

Plenty of people despise money – few are able to give it away.
– Duc de La Rochefoucauld
  (1613-80)
  Maxims

Money is like a sixth sense, without which you cannot make a complete use of the other five.
– Somerset Maugham (1874-1965)
  Of Human Bondage

Money is the seed of money, and the first guinea is sometimes more difficult to acquire than the second million.
– Jean Jacques Rousseau (1712-78)
  Discours sur l'Origine et le Fondement de l'Inégalité Parmi les Hommes

'Unsound' money means deceit, misrepresentation, breach of contract, injustice and in the end impoverishment, chaos, revolution, tyranny and dictatorship. It is a primary responsibility of Government in a free society to maintain a trustworthy monetary unit of account and medium of exchange.
– Walter H. Salomon (1906-   )
  Evidence submitted to the Committee on the Monetary and Credit System, September, 1957

Money is indeed the most important thing in the world; and all sound and successful personal and national morality should have this fact for its basis.
– George Bernard Shaw
  (1856-1950)
  The Irrational Knot

Lack of money is the root of all evil.
– George Bernard Shaw
  (1856-1950)
  Man and Superman: Maxims for Revolutionists

Money is the most important thing in the world. It represents health, strength, honour, generosity, and beauty as conspicuously as the want of it represents illness, weakness, disgrace, meanness, and ugliness.
– George Bernard Shaw

(1856-1950)
Major Barbara: Preface

MORAL INDIGNATION

Moral indignation is jealousy with a
halo.
- H.G. Wells (1866-1946)
  The Wife of Sir Isaac Harman

MORAL STANDARDS

As for China's old moral standards,
they are not yet lost sight of by the
people of China. First come Loyalty
and Filial Devotion, then Kindness
and Love, then Faithfulness and
Justice, then Harmony and Peace.
- Dr Sun Yat-Sen (1866-1925)
  Speech, 2 March 1924

MORALITY

It is more moral to be behind the age
than in advance of it.
- Samuel Butler (1835-1902)
  Note Books

Morality turns on whether the
pleasure precedes the pain or follows
it (provided it is sufficient). Thus it is
immoral to get drunk because the
headache comes after the drinking,
but if the headache came first and
the drunkenness afterwards, it would
be moral to get drunk.
- Samuel Butler (1835-1902)
  Ibid.

Foundations of morality are like all
other foundations; if you dig too
much about them the superstructure
will come tumbling down.

- Samuel Butler
  Ibid.

In cases of doubtful morality, it is
usual to say, is there any harm in
doing this? This question may
sometimes be best answered by
asking ourselves another; is there
any harm in letting it alone?
- Reverend C.C. Colton
  (1780?-1832)
  Lacon

We know of no spectacle so
ridiculous as the British public in
one of its periodical fits of morality.
- Lord Macaulay (1800-59)
  *Essays: Moore's Life of
  Lord Byron*

Wherever there is an ascendant class,
a large portion of the morality of the
country emanates from its class
interests, and its feelings of class
superiority.
- John Stuart Mill (1806-73)
  On Liberty

Morality is the herd-instinct in the
individual.
- Friedrich Nietzsche (1844-1900)
  Die Fröhliche Wissenschaft

Morality knows nothing of
geographical boundaries or
distinctions of race.
- Herbert Spencer (1820-1903)
  Social Statics

MOTHERS

. . . despise not thy mother when she
is old.
- *Bible*, Authorized version
  Proverbs, Ch. 23, v. 22

MOTHERS-IN-LAW

Go not empty unto thy mother in law.
- *Bible*, Authorized version
  Ruth, Ch. 3, v. 17

MOTIVES

My means are sane, my motive and my object mad.
- Herman Melville (1819-91)
  Moby Dick

MOUNTAINS

Mountains are the beginning and the end of all natural scenery.
- John Ruskin (1819-1900)
  Modern Painters

MURDER

. . . murder cannot be hid long. . .
- William Shakespeare (1564-1616)
  The Merchant of Venice, Act II,
  Sc. II

MURDERERS

Every murderer is probably somebody's old friend.
- Agatha Christie (1890-1976)
  The Mysterious Affair at Styles

MUSIC

Music has charms to sooth a savage beast.
- William Congreve (1670-1729)
  The Mourning Bride, Act I

Music is nothing else but wild sounds civilized into time and tune.
- Thomas Fuller (1608-61)
  The History of the Worthies of England

In the judgment of Reason music has less worth than any other of the beautiful arts.
- Immanuel Kant (1724-1804)
  Critique of Judgment

Musick is the thing of the world that I love most.
- Samuel Pepys (1633-1703)
  Diary, 30 July 1666

MUSIC CRITICS

I had another dream the other day about music critics. They were small and rodent-like with padlocked ears, as if they had stepped out of a painting by Goya.
- Igor Stravinsky (1882-1971)
  London Evening Standard,
  29 October 1969

NATIONALITY

Our true nationality is mankind.
- H.G. Wells (1866-1946)
  The Outline of History

NATIONS

Nations, like men, have their infancy.
- Henry St John, Viscount
  Bolingbroke (1678-1751)
  On The Study and Use of History

Every nation, big or small, has its strong and weak points.

– Mao Tse-tung (1893-1976)
  Opening Address, Eighth National
  Congress of the Communist Party
  of China, 15 September 1956

NATURAL ENVIRONMENT

The problem which confronts Europe
and indeed the whole world, is to
decide what restrictions are necessary
to protect our natural environment
from our own exploitation.
– HRH Prince Philip, Duke of
  Edinburgh (1921-   )
  Speech, European Conservation
  Year 1970 Conference,
  Strasbourg, 9 February 1970

NATURE

Nature and man can never be fast
friends.
– Matthew Arnold (1822-88)
  In Harmony with Nature

There is no forgiveness in nature.
– Ugo Betti (1892-1953)
  Goat Island

Nature is but a name for an effect
Whose cause is God.
– William Cowper (1731-1800)
  The Task

Nature is the art of God.
– Dante (1265-1321)
  De Monarchia

NECESSITY

Necessity is the plea for every
infringement of human freedom. It is
the argument of tyrants; it is the

creed of slaves.
– William Pitt (1759-1806)
  Speech, House of Commons,
  18 November 1783

NEGLECT

Art quickens Nature; Care will make
  a face:
Neglected beauty perisheth apace.
– Robert Herrick (1591-1674)
  Hesperides: Neglect

Self-love, my liege, is not so vile a sin
As self-neglecting.
– William Shakespeare (1564-1616)
  King Henry V, Act II, Sc. IV

NEGOTIATION

The stronger never treat, they dictate
the terms which the weak obey.
– Napoleon Bonaparte (1769-1821)
  *Political Aphorisms, Moral and
  Philosophical Thoughts of the
  Emperor Napoleon*, collected by
  Cte. Ate. G. De Liancourt

Let us never negotiate out of fear.
But let us never fear to negotiate.
– John F. Kennedy (1917-63)
  Inaugural Address,
  20 January 1961

NEIGHBOURS

Love thy Neighbour; yet don't pull
down your Hedge.
– Benjamin Franklin (1706-90)
  Poor Richard's Almanack, 1754

NEW RULE

Should anyone become the ruler either of a city or of a state, especially if he has no sure footing in it . . . the best thing he can do in order to retain such a principality, given that he be a new prince, is to organise everything in that state afresh; e.g. in its cities to appoint new governors, with new titles and new authority, the governors themselves being new men; to make the rich poor and the poor rich . . . as well as to build new cities, to destroy those already built, and to move the inhabitants from one place to another far distant from it; in short, to leave nothing of that province intact, and nothing in it, neither rank, nor institution, nor form of government, nor wealth, except that it be held by such as recognise that it comes from you.
— Niccolo Machiavelli (1469-1527)
   Discourses

NEWS

News is what a chap who doesn't care much about anything wants to read. And it's only news until he's read it. After that it's dead.
— Evelyn Waugh (1903-66)
   Scoop

NEWSPAPERS

Nowhere else can one find so miscellaneous, so various, an amount of knowledge as is contained in a good newspaper.
— Henry Ward Beecher (1813-87)
   Proverbs from Plymouth Pulpit

Were it left to me to decide whether we should have a government without newspapers, or newspapers without a government, I should not hesitate a moment to prefer the latter.
— Thomas Jefferson (1743-1826)
   Letter to Col. Edward Carrington,
   16 January 1787

The man who never looks into a newspaper is better informed than he who reads them; inasmuch as he who knows nothing is nearer to truth than he whose mind is filled with falsehood and errors.
— Thomas Jefferson (1743-1826)
   Letter to John Norvell,
   11 June 1807

Newspapers always excite curiosity. No one ever lays one down without a feeling of disappointment.
— Charles Lamb (1775-1834)
   Last Essays of Elia: Detached Thoughts on Books and Reading

NOBILITY

New nobility is but the act of power; but ancient nobility is the act of time.
— Francis Bacon (1561-1626)
   Essays: Of Nobility

NOISE

. . . it is impossible to imagine a more scroobious and unpleasant sound than that caused by the simultaneous sneezing of many millions of angry Mice.
— Edward Lear (1812-88)
   The Story of the Four Little

*Children who went Round
the World*

NONSENSE

A little nonsense now and then,
is relished by the wisest men.
— Roald Dahl (1916-   )
    *Charlie and the Great Glass
    Elevator*

NOSE

A great nose indicates a great man —
Genial, courteous, intellectual,
Virile, courageous.
— Edmond Rostand (1868-1918)
    Cyrano de Bergerac

NOVELISTS

Novelists should never allow
themselves to weary of the study of
real life.
— Charlotte Brontë (1816-55)
    The Professor

NOVELS

Novel, n. A short story padded.
— Ambrose Bierce (1842-1914?)
    The Devil's Dictionary

A good novel tells us the truth about
its hero; but a bad novel tells us the
truth about its author.
— G.K. Chesterton (1874-1936)
    Heretics

The only obligation to which in
advance we may hold a novel without
incurring the accusation of being

arbitrary, is that it be interesting.
— Henry James (1843-1916)
    The Art of Fiction

Make 'em laugh; make 'em cry; make
'em wait.
— Charles Reade (1814-84)
    Recipe for a Successful Novel

NOVEMBER

November is the most disagreeable
month in the whole year.
— Louisa May Alcott (1832-88)
    Little Women

NUCLEAR WEAPONS

The tremendous menace of this day
and age is not the stockpile of
nuclear weapons which human
ingenuity has devised, but the grim
fact that the men in charge of them
are as mediocre as those who
invented them are brilliant.
— Peter Ustinov (1921-   )
    Rectorial Address, University of
    Dundee, 17 October 1968

NYMPHETS

Between the age limits of nine and
fourteen there occur maidens who, to
certain bewitched travellers, twice or
many times older than they, reveal
their nature, which is not human, but
nymphic (that is, demoniac); and
these chosen creatures I propose to
designate as 'nymphets'.
— Vladimir Nabokov (1899-1977)
    Lolita

OATS

oats. A grain, which in England is generally given to horses, but in Scotland supports the people.
— Samuel Johnson (1709-84)
   Dictionary

OBEDIENCE

Let thy Child's first lesson be Obedience, and the second will be what thou wilt.
— Benjamin Franklin (1706-90)
   Poor Richard's Almanack, 1739

OBSCURITY

Obscurity often brings safety.
— Aesop (*c.* 550 BC)
   The Tree and the Road

OBSERVATION

Innocent and infinite are the pleasures of observation.
— Henry James (1843-1916)
   The Middle Years

OCTOBER

. . . October, that ambiguous month, the month of tension, the unendurable month.
— Doris Lessing (1919-   )
   A Proper Marriage

OLD

I love everything that's old; old friends, old times, old manners, old books, old wines.
— Oliver Goldsmith (1728-74)
   She Stoops to Conquer, Act I

OPENING CEREMONIES

There are many things which we do which don't seem to have any particular point or tangible result. Take today; a lot of time and energy has been spent on arranging for you to listen to me take a long time to declare open a building which everybody knows is open already.
— HRH Prince Philip, Duke of Edinburgh (1921-   )
   Speech, opening of Chesterfield College of Technology, England, 21 November 1958

OPINIONS

When the man you like switches from what he said a year ago, or four years ago, he is a broadminded person who has courage enough to change his mind with changing conditions. When a man you don't like does it, he is a liar who has broken his promises.
— Franklin P. Adams (1881-1960)
   Nods and Becks

The more securely a man holds an opinion the more temperate he can afford to be, and the more temperate he is the more weight he will carry with those who are in the long run weightiest.
— Samuel Butler (1835-1902)
   Note Books

Every new opinion, at its starting, is precisely in a minority of one.

— Thomas Carlyle (1795-1881)
On Heroes and Hero-Worship

I am always of the opinion with the learned, if they speak first.
— William Congreve (1670-1729)
Incognita

Time and circumstance, which enlarge the views of most men, narrow the views of women almost invariably.
— Thomas Hardy (1840-1928)
Jude the Obscure

When any opinion leads to absurdity, it is certainly false; but it is not certain that an opinion is false because it is of dangerous consequence.
— David Hume (1711-76)
An Enquiry Concerning Human Understanding

New opinions are always suspected, and usually opposed, without any other reason but because they are not already common.
— John Locke (1632-1704)
Essay Concerning Human Understanding

No one pretends that actions should be as free as opinions. On the contrary, even opinions lose their immunity when the circumstances in which they are expressed are such as to constitute their expression a positive instigation to some mischievous act.
— John Stuart Mill (1806-73)
On Liberty

He who knows only his own side of the case, knows little of that. His reasons may be good, and no one may have been able to refute them. But if he is equally unable to refute the reasons on the opposite side; if he does not so much as know what they are, he has no ground for preferring either opinion.
— John Stuart Mill
Ibid.

A person who derives all his instructions from teachers or books, even if he escape the besetting temptation of contenting himself with cram, is under no compulsion to hear both sides; accordingly it is far from a frequent accomplishment, even among thinkers, to know both sides; and the weakest part of what everybody says in defence of his opinion is what he intends as a reply to antagonists.
— John Stuart Mill
Ibid.

. . . the majority of the eminent men of every past generation held many opinions now known to be erroneous, and did or approved numerous things which no one will now justify.
— John Stuart Mill
Ibid.

Popular opinions, on subjects not palpable to sense, are often true, but seldom or never the whole truth.
— John Stuart Mill
Ibid.

Opinion in good men is but knowledge in the making.
— John Milton (1608-74)
Areopagitica

One often contradicts an opinion when it is really only the tone in which it has been presented that is

unsympathetic.
- Friedrich Nietzsche (1844-1900)
  Human, All Too Human

... I have bought
Golden opinions from all sorts of
  people ...
- William Shakespeare (1564-1616)
  Macbeth, Act I, Sc. VII

Opinion is ultimately determined by
the feelings, and not by the intellect.
- Herbert Spencer (1820-1903)
  Social Statics

OPPORTUNITIES

A man must make his opportunity, as
oft as find it.
- Francis Bacon (1561-1626)
  Advancement of Learning

A wise Man will make more
Opportunities than he finds.
- Thomas Fuller (1654-1734)
  Gnomologia

Wealth in modern societies is
distributed according to opportunity;
and while opportunity depends
partly upon talent and energy, it
depends still more upon birth, social
position, access to education and
inherited wealth; in a word, upon
property.
- Richard H. Tawney (1880-1962)
  The Acquisitive Society .

OPPOSITION

He that is not with me is against me.
- *Bible*, Authorized version
  St Matthew, Ch. 12, v. 30

No Government can be long secure
without a formidable Opposition.
- Benjamin Disraeli (1804-81)
  Coningsby

OPTIMISTS

The optimist proclaims that we live
in the best of all possible worlds; and
the pessimist fears this is true.
- James Branch Cabell (1879-1958)
  The Silver Stallion

The place where optimism most
flourishes is the lunatic asylum.
- Havelock Ellis (1859-1939)
  The Dance of Life

Many of the optimists in the world
don't own a hundred dollars, and
because of their optimism never will.
- Edgar Watson Howe (1853-1937)
  The Blessing of Business

The man who is a pessimist before
forty-eight knows too much; if he is
an optimist after it, he knows too
little.
- Mark Twain (1835-1910)
  Notebook

OVER-CONFIDENCE

Over-confidence invites danger.
- Pierre Corneille (1606-84)
  Le Cid

OVER-POPULATION

Creation destroys as it goes, throws
down one tree for the rise of another.
But ideal mankind would abolish
death, multiply itself million upon

million, rear up city upon city, save every parasite alive, until the accumulation of mere existence is swollen to a horror.
— D.H. Lawrence (1885-1930)
  St Mawr

Population, when unchecked, increases in a geometrical ratio. Subsistence increases only in an arithmetical ratio. A slight acquaintance with numbers will show the immensity of the first power in comparison of the second.
— Thomas Robert Malthus (1766-1834)
  An Essay on the Principle of Population

... in a country either over-peopled, or threatened with being so, to produce children, beyond a very small number, with the effect of reducing the reward of labour by their competition, is a serious offence against all who live by the remuneration of their labour.
— John Stuart Mill (1806-73)
  On Liberty

OVERTHROW

They, that fear an Overthrow, are half beaten.
— Thomas Fuller (1654-1734)
  Gnomologia

PACIFISTS

The pacifists' task today is to find a method of helping and healing which provides a revolutionary constructive substitute for war.

— Vera Brittain (1893-1970)
  The Rebel Passion

PAPERWORK

The man whose life is devoted to paperwork has lost the initiative. He is dealing with things that are brought to his notice, having ceased to notice anything for himself. He has been essentially defeated in his job.
— C. Northcote Parkinson (1909-   )
  In-Laws and Outlaws

PARDON

Pardoning the Bad, is injuring the Good.
— Benjamin Franklin (1706-90)
  Poor Richard's Almanack, 1748

PARENTAGE

Parentage is a very important profession; but no test of fitness for it is ever imposed in the interests of children.
— George Bernard Shaw (1856-1950)
  Everybody's Political What's What

PARENTS

If you have never been hated by your child, you have never been a parent.
— Bette Davis (1908-   )
  The Lonely Life

People are always rather bored with their parents. That's human nature.
— Somerset Maugham

115

(1874-1965)
The Bread-Winner, Act II

Children begin by loving their parents; after a time they judge them; rarely, if ever, do they forgive them.
— Oscar Wilde (1854-1900)
    A Woman of No Importance, Act I

PARLEY

Neither a Fortress nor a Maidenhead will hold out long after they begin to parley.
— Benjamin Franklin (1706-90)
    Poor Richard's Almanack, 1734

PARLIAMENT

A Parliament is nothing less than a big meeting of more or less idle people.
— Walter Bagehot (1826-77)
    The English Constitution

PARTING

Parting is such sweet sorrow.
— William Shakespeare (1564-1616)
    Romeo and Juliet, Act II, Sc. II

PARTISANSHIP

Partisanship is our great curse. We too readily assume that everything has two sides and that it is our duty to be on one side or the other.
— James Harvey Robinson (1863-1936)
    The Mind in the Making

PASSION

If *Passion* drives, let *Reason* hold the Reins.
— Benjamin Franklin (1706-90)
    Poor Richard's Almanack, 1749

Where Passion is high, there Reason is low.
— Thomas Fuller (1654-1734)
    Gnomologia

PASSIONS

Three passions, simple but overwhelmingly strong, have governed my life: the longing for love, the search for knowledge, and unbearable pity for the suffering of mankind.
— Bertrand Russell (1872-1970)
    Autobiography

PAST

Why doesn't the past decently bury itself, instead of sitting waiting to be admired by the present?
— D.H. Lawrence (1885-1930)
    St Mawr

. . . what's past is prologue . . .
— William Shakespeare (1564-1616)
    The Tempest, Act II, Sc. I

PATIENCE

He that can have Patience, can have what he will.
— Benjamin Franklin (1706-90)
    Poor Richard's Almanack, 1736

Patience, that blending of moral courage with physical timidity.
— Thomas Hardy (1840-1928)
Tess of the D'Urbervilles

Patience is the best remedy for every trouble.
— Plautus (254-184 BC)
Rudens, Act II

PATRIOT

Patriot, n. One to whom the interests of a part seem superior to those of the whole. The dupe of statesmen and the tool of conquerors.
— Ambrose Bierce (1842-1914?)
The Devil's Dictionary

A patriot is a fool in ev'ry age.
— Alexander Pope (1688-1744)
Imitations of Horace: Epilogue to the Satires

PATRIOTISM

Patriotism is the last refuge of a scoundrel.
— Samuel Johnson (1709-84)
Boswell's Life of Johnson

Patriotism is a kind of religion; it is the egg from which wars are hatched.
— Guy de Maupassant (1850-93)
My Uncle Sosthenes

PATRON

patron. One who countenances, supports or protects. Commonly a wretch who supports with insolence, and is paid with flattery.

— Samuel Johnson (1709-84)
Dictionary

PATRONIZING

A patronizing disposition always has its meaner side.
— George Eliot (1819-80)
Adam Bede

PEACE

Peace, n. In international affairs, a period of cheating between two periods of fighting.
— Ambrose Bierce (1842-1914?)
The Devil's Dictionary

An unjust peace is better than a just war.
— Cicero (106-43 BC)
Ad Atticum

Nothing can bring you peace but yourself.
— Ralph Waldo Emerson (1803-82)
Essays: Self-Reliance

The most disadvantageous peace is better than the most just war.
— Desiderius Erasmus (1466?-1536)
Adagia

There never was a good war or a bad peace.
— Benjamin Franklin (1706-90)
Letter to Josiah Quincy,
11 September 1773

Peace is a daily, a weekly, a monthly process, gradually changing opinions, slowly eroding old barriers, quietly building new structures.
— John F. Kennedy (1917-63)

Address to United Nations
General Assembly,
20 September 1963

Peace, like war, can succeed only
where there is a will to enforce it,
and where there is available power to
enforce it.
— Franklin Delano Roosevelt
(1882-1945)
Speech, Foreign Policy
Association, New York City,
21 October 1944

Making peace is harder than making
war.
— Adlai Stevenson (1900-65)
Address to Chicago Council on
Foreign Relations, 22 March 1946

They have not wanted *Peace* at all;
they have wanted to be spared war —
as though the absence of war was the
same as peace.
— Dorothy Thompson (1894-1961)
On The Record, May, 1958

To be prepared for war is one of the
most effectual means of preserving
peace.
— George Washington (1732-99)
Speech to Congress,
8 January 1790

Peach hath higher tests of manhood
Than battle ever knew.
— John Greenleaf Whittier
(1807-92)
The Hero

PEACEMAKERS

. . . blessed are the peacemakers on
earth.
— William Shakespeare (1564-1616)

King Henry VI, Pt. II, Act II,
Sc. I

PEDANTS

Plague take all your pedants, say I!
— Robert Browning (1812-89)
Sibrandus Schafraburgensis

pedant. (1) A schoolmaster. (2) A
man vain of low knowledge; a man
awkwardly ostentatious of his
literature.
— Samuel Johnson (1709-84)
Dictionary

PEERAGE

You should study the Peerage . . . It
is the one book a young man about
town should know thoroughly, and it
is the best thing in fiction the English
have done.
— Oscar Wilde (1854-1900)
A Woman of No Importance,
Act III

PENSION

pension. An allowance made to any
one without an equivalent. In
England it is generally understood to
mean pay given to a state hireling for
treason to his country.
— Samuel Johnson (1709-84)
Dictionary

PEOPLE

It was no wonder that people were so
horrible when they started life as
children.

– Kingsley Amis (1922-)
  One Fat Englishman

People on the whole are very simple-minded in whatever country one finds them. They are so simple as to take literally, more often than not, the things their leaders tell them.
– Pearl S. Buck (1892-1973)
  What America Means to Me

There are people who resemble popular songs – they are sung for a time and then forgotten.
– Duc de La Rochefoucauld (1613-80)
  Maxims

It is absurd to divide people into good and bad. People are either charming or tedious.
– Oscar Wilde (1854-1900)
  Lady Windermere's Fan, Act I

Most people are other people. Their thoughts are someone else's opinions, their lives a mimicry, their passions a quotation.
– Oscar Wilde (1854-1900)
  'Phrases and Philosophies for the Use of the Young', *Chameleon*, December, 1894

PEOPLE'S WILL

. . . I promise that the general will of the people shall ever be my supreme law, and that the people's will shall guide me in all my actions . .
– Simon Bolivar (1783-1830)
  Speech made to Venezuelan Assembly, Caracas, 2 January 1814

PERFECTION

The pursuit of perfection, then, is the pursuit of sweetness and light.
– Matthew Arnold (1822-88)
  Culture and Anarchy

PERSUASION

Reasonable men are open to persuasion.
– Plutarch (46-120)
  Moralia

The silence often of pure innocence
Persuades when speaking fails.
– William Shakespeare (1564-1616)
  The Winter's Tale, Act II, Sc. II

PHILANTHROPY

Philanthropy is commendable, but it must not cause the philanthropist to overlook the circumstances of economic injustice which make philanthropy necessary.
– Martin Luther King (1929-68)
  Strength to Love

Philanthropy is almost the only virtue which is sufficiently appreciated by mankind.
– Henry David Thoreau (1817-62)
  Walden

PHILOSOPHERS

There is nothing so absurd but some philosopher has said it.
– Cicero (106-43 BC)
  De Divinatione

Philosophy / Plays

A great memory does not make a philosopher, any more than a dictionary can be called a grammar.
- Cardinal Newman (1801-90)
  The Idea of a University

There are now-a-days professors of philosophy but not philosophers.
- Henry David Thoreau (1817-62)
  Walden

PHILOSOPHY

All good moral philosophy is but an handmaid to religion.
- Francis Bacon (1561-1626)
  Advancement of Learning

Philosophy is not a body of doctrine, but an activity.
- Ludwig Wittgenstein (1889-1951)
  Tractatus Logico-philosophicus

PHYSICIANS

The competent physician, before he attempts to give medicine to his patient, makes himself acquainted not only with the disease which he wishes to cure, but also with the habits and constitution of the sick man.
- Cicero (106-43 BC)
  De Oratore

He's the best physician that knows the worthlessness of the most medicines.
- Benjamin Franklin (1706-90)
  Poor Richard's Almanack, 1733

PITY

Pity is but one remove from love.
- Samuel Richardson (1689-1761)
  Sir Charles Grandison

PLANS

Where young boys plan for what they will achieve and attain, young girls plan for whom they will achieve and attain.
- Charlotte Perkins Gilman (1860-1935)
  Women and Economics

It is a bad plan that cannot be changed.
- Publilius Syrus
  (*c*. 1st century BC)
  Maxims

PLAYS

A play ought to be a just and lively image of human nature, representing its passions and humours, and the changes of fortune to which it is subject, for the delight and instruction of mankind.
- John Dryden (1631-1700)
  Of Dramatic Poesy

Popular Stage-plays are sinful, heathenish, lewd, ungodly Spectacles, and most pernicious Corruptions; condemned in all ages, as intolerable Mischiefs to Churches, to Republics, to the manners, minds and souls of men.
- William Prynne (1600-69)
  Histriomastix

PLAYTHINGS

Old Boys have their Playthings as
well as young Ones; the Difference is
only in the Price.
- Benjamin Franklin (1706-90)
  Poor Richard's Almanack, 1752

PLEASURE

One half of the world cannot
understand the pleasures of the other.
- Jane Austen (1775-1817)
  Emma

The Pleasures of the Rich are bought
with the Tears of the Poor.
- Thomas Fuller (1654-1734)
  Gnomologia

There is no such thing as pure
pleasure — some anxiety always goes
with it.
- Ovid (43 BC-17 AD)
  Metamorphoses

Reason's whole pleasure, all the joys
  of Sense,
Lie in three words, Health, Peace,
  and Competence.
- Alexander Pope (1688-1744)
  An Essay on Man

Pleasure is the only thing one should
live for. Nothing ages like happiness.
- Oscar Wilde (1854-1900)
  'Phrases and Philosophies for the
  Use of the Young', *Chameleon*,
  December, 1894

PLOTS

. . . our plot is as good a plot as ever
was laid; our friends true and
constant: a good plot, good friends,
and full of expectation; an excellent
plot, very good friends.
- William Shakespeare (1564-1616)
  King Henry IV, Pt. I, Act II,
  Sc. III

POETRY

Poetry is simply the most beautiful,
impressive and widely effective mode
of saying things, and hence its
importance.
- Matthew Arnold (1822-88)
  Essays in Criticism

Poetry's unnat'ral; no man ever
talked poetry 'cept a beadle on
boxin' day.
- Charles Dickens (1812-70)
  Pickwick Papers

Poetry should be great and
unobtrusive, a thing which enters
into one's soul, and does not startle
it or amaze it with itself, but with its
subject.
- John Keats (1795-1821)
  Letter to J.H. Reynolds,
  3 February 1818

If Poetry comes not as naturally as
the Leaves to a tree it had better not
come at all.
- John Keats (1795-1821)
  Letter to John Taylor,
  27 February 1818

The immortality of poetry is worth
the sweat of noblemen.
- Friedrich Gottlieb Klopstock
  (1724-1803)
  Lake Zurich

Poetry / Poets

A poem should not mean
But be.
— Archibald MacLeish (1892-)
  Ars Poetica

It is easier to write a mediocre poem
than to understand a good one.
— Michel Eyquem de Montaigne
  (1533-92)
  Essays

Poetry is an act of peace. Peace goes
into the making of a poet as flour
goes into the making of bread.
— Pablo Neruda (1904-73)
  Confieso Que He Vivido:
  Memorias

Poetry comes fine-spun from a mind
at peace.
— Ovid (43 BC-17 AD)
  Tristia

Science is for those who learn;
poetry, for those who know.
— Joseph Roux (1834-86)
  Meditations of a Parish Priest

What is poetry? The suggestion, by
the imagination, of noble grounds for
the noble sentiments.
— John Ruskin (1819-1900)
  Modern Painters

Poetry is the record of the best and
happiest moments of the happiest
and best minds.
— Percy Bysshe Shelley (1792-1822)
  A Defence of Poetry

Poetry lifts the veil from the hidden
beauty of the world, and makes
familiar objects be as if they were not
familiar.
— Percy Bysshe Shelley
  Ibid.

We have been able to have fine
poetry in England because the public
do not read it, and consequently do
not influence it.
— Oscar Wilde (1854-1900)
  The Soul of Man Under Socialism

Poetry is the breath and finer spirit
of all knowledge; it is the
impassioned expression which is in
the countenance of all science.
— William Wordsworth (1770-1850)
  Lyrical Ballads

Poetry is the spontaneous overflow
of powerful feelings: it takes its
origin from emotion recollected in
tranquillity.
— William Wordsworth
  Ibid.

POETS

A poet is, before anything else, a
person who is passionately in love
with language.
— W.H. Auden (1907-73)
  The New York Times,
  9 October 1960

I agree with one of your reputable
critics that a taste for drawing-rooms
has spoiled more poets than ever did
a taste for gutters.
— Thomas Beer (1889-1940)
  The Mauve Decade

All poets are mad.
— Robert Burton (1577-1640)
  The Anatomy of Melancholy

No man was ever yet a great poet,
without being at the same time a
profound philosopher.
— Samuel Taylor Coleridge

(1772-1834)
Biographia Literaria

All poets pretend to write for immortality, but the whole tribe have no objection to present pay and present praise.
— Reverend C.C. Colton
(1780?-1832)
Lacon

A very good or very bad Poet is remarkable; but a middling one, who can bear?
— Thomas Fuller (1654-1734)
Gnomologia

Poets utter great and wise things which they do not themselves understand.
— Plato (*c.* 428-348 BC)
Republic

He who draws noble delights from the sentiments of poetry is a true poet, though he has never written a line in all his life.
— George Sand (1804-76)
The Haunted Pool

Poets are the unacknowledged legislators of the world.
— Percy Bysshe Shelley (1792-1822)
A Defence of Poetry

Every good poet includes a critic, but the reverse will not hold.
— William Shenstone (1714-63)
On Writing and Books

A poet looks at the world as a man looks at a woman.
— Wallace Stevens (1879-1955)
Opus Posthumous: Adagia

A poet can survive everything but a misprint.
— Oscar Wilde (1854-1900)
The Children of the Poets

POLICEMEN

A policeman's lot is not a happy one.
— W.S. Gilbert (1836-1911)
The Pirates of Penzance

POLITENESS

Politeness, n. The most acceptable hypocrisy.
— Ambrose Bierce (1842-1914?)
The Devil's Dictionary

Politeness is organized indifference.
— Paul Valéry (1871-1945)
Tel Quel

POLITICAL PARTIES

All political parties die at last of swallowing their own lies.
— John Arbuthnot (1667-1735)
Epigram

There is no act of treachery or meanness of which a political party is not capable; for in politics there is no honour.
— Benjamin Disraeli (1804-81)
Vivian Grey

In politics, again, it is almost a commonplace, that a party of order or stability, and a party of progress or reform, are both necessary elements of a healthy state of political life; until the one or the other shall have so enlarged its

Political Parties / Politics

mental grasp as to be a party equally of order and of progress, knowing and distinguishing what is fit to be preserved from what ought to be swept away.
— John Stuart Mill (1806-73)
  On Liberty

POLITICIANS

Persistence in one opinion has never been considered a merit in political leaders.
— Cicero (106-43 BC)
  Ad Familiares

A politician is a man who understands government, and it takes a politician to run a government. A statesman is a politician who's been dead 10 or 15 years.
— Harry S. Truman (1884-1972)
  New York World Telegram & Sun,
  12 April 1958

POLITICS

Politics, n. A strife of interests masquerading as a contest of principles. The conduct of public affairs for private advantage.
— Ambrose Bierce (1842-1914?)
  The Devil's Dictionary

Politics are usually the executive expression of human immaturity.
— Vera Brittain (1893-1970)
  The Rebel Passion

What is politics but persuading the public to vote for this and support that and endure these for the promise of those?
— Gilbert Highet (1906-78)

'The Art of Persuasion',
Vogue, January, 1951

Politics has its virtues, all too many of them — it would not rank with baseball as a topic of conversation if it did not satisfy a good many things — but one can suspect that its secret appeal is close to nicotine.
— Norman Mailer (1923-)
  The Presidential Papers

The whole aim of practical politics is to keep the populace alarmed (and hence clamorous to be led to safety) by an endless series of hobgoblins.
— H.L. Mencken (1880-1956)
  In Defense of Women

Those who would treat politics and morality apart will never understand the one or the other.
— Lord Morley (Viscount Morley of Blackburn) (1838-1923)
  Rousseau

In politics, there is a wide difference between promises and reality.
— Napoleon Bonaparte (1769-1821)
  Political Aphorisms, Moral and Philosophical Thoughts of the Emperor Napoleon, collected by Cte. Ate. G. De Liancourt

Politics is perhaps the only profession for which no preparation is thought necessary.
— Robert Louis Stevenson (1850-94)
  Familiar Studies of Men and Books

POOR

Four spectres haunt the Poor — Old Age, Accident, Sickness and Unemployment.
— David Lloyd George (1863-1945)
   Speech, Reading, England,
   1 January 1910

There is only one class in the community that thinks more about money than the rich, and that is the poor.
— Oscar Wilde (1854-1900)
   The Soul of Man Under Socialism

POPULAR OPINION

Popular Opinion is the greatest Lie in the World.
— Thomas Fuller (1654-1734)
   Gnomologia

POPULARITY

Popularity is a crime from the moment it is sought; it is only a virtue where men have it whether they will or no.
— Sir George Savile (1633-95)
   Moral Thoughts and Reflections

POPULATION

If, then, you want to have a large population and to provide it with arms so as to establish a great empire, you will have made your population such that you cannot now handle it as you please. While, if you keep it either small or unarmed so as to be able to manage it, and then acquire dominions, either you will lose your

hold on it or it will become so debased that you will be at the mercy of anyone who attacks you.
— Niccolo Machiavelli (1469-1527)
   Discourses

POSITIONS

Citizens who have held Higher Posts should not disdain to accept Lower.
— Niccolo Machiavelli (1469-1527)
   Discourses

POSSIBILITIES

All things are possible until they are proved impossible — and even the impossible may only be so, as of now.
— Pearl S. Buck (1892-1973)
   A Bridge for Passing

POVERTY

Poverty is an anomaly to rich people. It is very difficult to make out why people who want dinner do not ring the bell.
— Walter Bagehot (1826-77)
   Literary Studies

Having been poor is no shame, but being ashamed of it, is.
— Benjamin Franklin (1706-90)
   Poor Richard's Almanack, 1749

A light Purse makes a heavy Heart.
— Thomas Fuller (1654-1734)
   Gnomologia

An empty Purse frights away Friends.
— Thomas Fuller
   Ibid.

Poverty is no sin.
- George Herbert (1593-1633)
  Jacula Prudentum

Oh! poverty is a weary thing 'tis full
  of grief and pain;
It keepeth down the soul of man, as
  with an iron chain.
- Mary Howitt (1799-1888)
  The Sale of the Pet Lamb

Few, save the poor, feel for the poor.
- Letitia Elizabeth Landon
  (1802-38)
  The Poor

Poverty, in any sense implying
suffering, may be completely
extinguished by the wisdom of
society, combined with the good
sense and providence of individuals.
- John Stuart Mill (1806-73)
  Utilitarianism

The greatest of evils and the worst of
crimes is poverty.
- George Bernard Shaw
  (1856-1950)
  Major Barbara

No society can surely be flourishing
and happy, of which the far greater
part of the members are poor and
miserable.
- Adam Smith (1723-90)
  The Wealth of Nations

POWER

He who has his thumb on the purse
has the power.
- Otto von Bismarck (1815-98)
  Speech, North German Reichstag,
  21 May 1869

Power gradually extirpates from the
mind every humane and gentle virtue.
- Edmund Burke (1729-97)
  A Vindication of Natural Society

The only prize much cared for by the
powerful is power. The prize of the
general is not a bigger tent, but
command.
- Oliver Wendell Holmes, Jr
  (1841-1935)
  Law and the Court

Unlimited power is apt to corrupt the
minds of those who possess it.
- William Pitt (1st Earl of Chatham)
  (1708-78)
  Speech in the House of Lords,
  9 January 1770

PRAISE

Let another man praise thee, and not
thine own mouth; a stranger, and not
thine own lips.
- *Bible*, Authorized version
  Proverbs, Ch. 27, v. 2

The advantage of doing one's praising
for oneself is that one can lay it on so
thick and exactly in the right places.
- Samuel Butler (1835-1902)
  The Way of All Flesh

The praise of a fool is more harmful
than his blame.
- Jean Pierre Claris Florian
  (1755-94)
  Fables

If you would reap Praise you must
  sow the Seeds,
Gentle Words and useful Deeds.
- Benjamin Franklin (1706-90)
  Poor Richard's Almanack, 1753

126

It is more difficult to praise rightly, than to blame.
- Thomas Fuller (1654-1734)
  Gnomologia

Praise makes good Men better, and bad Men worse.
- Thomas Fuller
  Ibid.

We usually only praise that we may be praised.
- Duc de La Rochefoucauld
  (1613-80)
  Maxims

I will praise any man that will praise me.
- William Shakespeare (1564-1616)
  Antony and Cleopatra, Act II,
  Sc. 6

PRAYER

He prayeth best who loveth best
All things both great and small.
- Samuel Taylor Coleridge
  (1772-1834)
  The Ancient Mariner

PREACHERS

A successful woman preacher was once asked 'what special obstacles have you met as a woman in the ministry?' 'Not one,' she answered, 'except the lack of a minister's wife.'
- Anna Garlin Spencer (1851-1931)
  Woman's Share in Social Culture

PREJUDICE

Prejudices, it is well known, are most difficult to eradicate from the heart whose soil has never been loosened or fertilized by education; they grow there, firm as weeds among stones.
- Charlotte Brontë (1816-55)
  Jane Eyre

Prejudice is the child of ignorance.
- William Hazlitt (1778-1830)
  Sketches and Essays

We all decry prejudice, yet are all prejudiced.
- Herbert Spencer (1820-1903)
  Social Statics

It is never too late to give up your prejudices.
- Henry David Thoreau (1817-62)
  Walden

Prejudice is the reasoning of the stupid.
- Voltaire (1694-1778)
  Sur la Loi Naturelle

PRESS

Freedom of the press is perhaps the freedom that has suffered the most from the gradual degradation of the idea of liberty.
- Albert Camus (1913-60)
  Resistance, Rebellion, and Death

A King of England has an interest in preserving the freedom of the press, because it is his interest to know the true state of the nation, which the courtiers would fain conceal, but of which a free press can alone inform him.

— Reverend C.C. Colton
  (1780?-1832)
  Lacon

What priestcraft was to the
fourteenth century, presscraft is
to the twentieth.
— William Graham Sumner
  (1840-1910)
  *The Forgotten Man and
  Other Essays*

PRIDE

Men often make the Mistake of
supposing that Pride is overcome
by Humility.
— Niccolo Machiavelli (1469-1527)
  Discourses

. . . my pride fell with my fortunes.
— William Shakespeare (1564-1616)
  As You Like It, Act I, Sc. II

PRINCIPLES

You can't learn too soon that the
most useful thing about a principle
is that it can always be sacrificed to
expediency.
— Somerset Maugham (1874-1965)
  The Circle, Act III

It is often easier to fight for
principles than to live up to them.
— Adlai Stevenson (1900-65)
  Speech, New York City,
  27 August 1952

PRISON

Prisons are built with stones of Law,
Brothels with bricks of Religion.

— William Blake (1757-1827)
  *The Marriage of Heaven and Hell:
  Proverbs of Hell*

Stone walls do not a prison make,
Nor iron bars a cage.
— Richard Lovelace (1618-58)
  To Althea, from Prison

PROBLEMS

I have yet to see any problem,
however complicated, which, when
you looked at it in the right way, did
not become still more complicated.
— Poul Anderson (1926-   )
  New Scientist,
  25 September 1969

Never let life's hardships disturb you.
After all, no one can avoid problems,
not even saints or sages.
— Nichiren Daishonin (1222-82)
  *The Major Writings of Nichiren
  Daishonin: Happiness in this
  World*

PROCRASTINATION

Procrastination is the thief of time.
— Edward Young (1683-1765)
  The Complaint: Night Thoughts

PROD

I am certainly not one of those who
need to be prodded. In fact, if
anything, I am a prod.
— Sir Winston Churchill
  (1874-1965)
  Speech, House of Commons,
  11 November 1942

PROFESSIONS

Of the professions it may be said that soldiers are becoming too popular, parsons too lazy, physicians too mercenary, and lawyers too powerful.
— Reverend C.C. Colton
    (1780?-1832)
    Lacon

All professions are conspiracies against the laity.
— George Bernard Shaw
    (1856-1950)
    The Doctor's Dilemma, Act I

PROFITS

The greater the skill deployed by governments in creating a climate of confidence and stability in which the industrial community believes it will earn and keep sufficient profit, the more dramatic will be the results.
— Michael Heseltine (1933-   )
    Speech, American Chamber of
    Commerce lunch, London,
    14 April 1976

PROGRESS

All progress is based upon a universal innate desire on the part of every organism to live beyond its income.
— Samuel Butler (1835-1902)
    Note Books

What we call 'Progress' is the exchange of one nuisance for another nuisance.
— Havelock Ellis (1859-1939)
    Impressions and Comments

People are the common denominator of progress.
— John Kenneth Galbraith (1908-   )
    Economic Development

So long as all the increased wealth which modern progress brings goes but to build up great fortunes, to increase luxury and make sharper the contrast between the House of Have and the House of Want, progress is not real and cannot be permanent.
— Henry George (1839-97)
    Progress and Poverty

The early difficulties in the way of spontaneous progress are so great, that there is seldom any choice of means for overcoming them; and a ruler full of the spirit of improvement is warranted in the use of any expedients that will attain an end, perhaps otherwise unattainable.
— John Stuart Mill (1806-73)
    On Liberty

A people, it appears, may be progressive for a certain length of time, and then stop: when does it stop? When it ceases to possess individuality.
— John Stuart Mill
    Ibid.

The reasonable man adapts himself to the world: the unreasonable one persists in trying to adapt the world to himself. Therefore all progress depends on the unreasonable man.
— George Bernard Shaw
    (1856-1950)
    *Man and Superman: Maxims
    for Revolutionists*

PROMISES

Men apt to promise, are apt to forget.
— Thomas Fuller (1654-1734)
  Gnomologia

Never promise more than you can perform.
— Publilius Syrus
  (*c*. 1st century BC)
  Maxims

A promise made is a debt unpaid.
— Robert William Service
  (1874-1958)
  The Cremation of Sam McGee

PROPAGANDA

The propagandist's purpose is to make one set of people forget that certain other sets of people are human.
— Aldous Huxley (1894-1963)
  The Olive Tree

There is no nonsense so arrant that it cannot be made the creed of the vast majority by adequate governmental action.
— Bertrand Russell (1872-1970)
  Unpopular Essays

Why is propaganda so much more successful when it stirs up hatred than when it tries to stir up friendly feeling?
— Bertrand Russell (1872-1970)
  The Conquest of Happiness

PROPERTY

The magic of property turns sand into gold.
— Arthur Young (1741-1820)
  Travels in France

Property has its duties as well as its rights.
— Thomas Drummond (1797-1840)
  Letter to the Earl of
  Donoughmore, 22 May 1838

PROSE

The poet gives us his essence, but prose takes the mould of the body and mind entire.
— Virginia Woolf (1882-1941)
  The Captain's Death Bed

PROSPERITY

Prosperity is only an instrument to be used, not a deity to be worshipped.
— Calvin Coolidge (1872-1933)
  Speech, Boston, Massachusetts,
  11 June 1928

Prosperity discovers Vice, Adversity Virtue.
— Benjamin Franklin (1706-90)
  Poor Richard's Almanack, 1751

PROVERBS

Proverbs are art — cheap art. As a general rule they are not true; unless indeed they happen to be mere platitudes.
— Joseph Conrad (1857-1924)
  Gaspar Ruiz

A proverb is much matter decocted into few words.
— Thomas Fuller (1608-61)

The History of the Worthies of England

Proverbs may not improperly be called the philosophy of the common people.
— James Howell (1594?-1666)
Proverbs

How often, when smarting under some unforeseen misfortune or disappointment, does a person call to mind some proverb or common saying, familiar to him all his life, the meaning of which, if he had ever before felt it as he does now, would have saved him from the calamity.
— John Stuart Mill (1806-73)
On Liberty

PRUDENCE

An ounce of prudence is worth a pound of gold.
— Tobias Smollett (1721-71)
Roderick Random

PSYCHIATRY

Psychiatry's chief contribution to philosophy is the discovery that the toilet is the seat of the soul.
— Alexander Chase (1926-   )
Perspectives

PUBLIC OPINION

There is nothing that makes more cowards and feeble men than public opinion.
— Henry Ward Beecher (1813-87)
Proverbs from Plymouth Pulpit

The public buys its opinions as it buys its meat, or takes in its milk, on the principle that it is cheaper to do this than to keep a cow. So it is, but the milk is more likely to be watered.
— Samuel Butler (1835-1902)
Note Books

There are times when public opinion is the worst of all opinions.
— Nicolas-Sébastien Chamfort (1741-94)
Maximes et Pensées

Public opinion, a vulgar, impertinent, anonymous tyrant who deliberately makes life unpleasant for anyone who is not content to be the average man.
— Dean Inge (1860-1954)
Outspoken Essays

Public opinion in this country is everything.
— Abraham Lincoln (1809-65)
Speech, Columbus, Ohio,
16 September 1859

Public opinion is a mysterious and invisible power, to which everything must yield. There is nothing more fickle, more vague, or more powerful; yet capricious as it is, it is nevertheless much more often true, reasonable, and just, than we imagine.
— Napoleon Bonaparte (1769-1821)
Political Aphorisms, Moral and Philosophical Thoughts of the Emperor Napoleon, collected by Cte. Ate. G. De Liancourt

PUBLIC SCHOOLS

Public schools are the nurseries of all vice and immorality.

Public Schools / Questions

— Henry Fielding (1707-54)
   Joseph Andrews

Anyone who has been to an English
public school will always feel
comparatively at home in prison.
— Evelyn Waugh (1903-66)
   Decline and Fall

PUBLICITY

Formerly, a public man needed a
private secretary for a barrier
between himself and the public.
Nowadays he has a *press* secretary,
to keep him properly in the public
eye.
— Daniel J. Boorstin (1914-   )
   The Image

PUNISHMENT

Man punishes the Action, but God
the intention.
— Thomas Fuller (1654-1734)
   Gnomologia

The refined punishments of the
spiritual mode are usually much more
indecent and dangerous than a good
smack.
— D.H. Lawrence (1885-1930)
   Fantasia of the Unconscious

We have no right, even as an example,
to put anyone to death unless it is
impossible to preserve him without
danger.
— Jean Jacques Rousseau (1712-78)
   Du Contrat Social

PURGATORY

There is no other purgatory but a
woman.
— Francis Beaumont (1584-1616)
   and John Fletcher (1579-1625)
   The Scornful Lady, Act III

PURITANS

A puritan is a person who pours
righteous indignation into the wrong
things.
— G.K. Chesterton (1874-1936)
   New York Times,
   21 November 1936

QUARRELS

Quarrels would not last long if the
fault were only on one side.
— Duc de La Rochefoucauld
   (1613-80)
   Maxims

For souls in growth, great quarrels
are great emancipations.
— Logan Pearsall Smith (1865-1946)
   Afterthoughts

The quarrels of lovers are the renewal
of love.
— Terence (*c*. 190-159 BC)
   Heauton Timoroumenos

QUESTIONS

Fools may ask more in an Hour, than
wise Men can answer in seven.
— Thomas Fuller (1654-1734)
   Gnomologia

He that nothing questioneth, nothing learneth.
- Thomas Fuller
  Ibid.

QUIET

She is as quiet as a Wasp in one's Ear.
- Thomas Fuller (1654-1734)
  Gnomologia

QUORUM

Quorum, n. A sufficient number of members of a deliberative body to have their own way and their own way of having it.
- Ambrose Bierce (1842-1914?)
  The Devil's Dictionary

QUOTATIONS

It is a good thing for an uneducated man to read books of quotations.
- Sir Winston Churchill
  (1874-1965)
  My Early Life

By necessity, by proclivity, and by delight, we all quote.
- Ralph Waldo Emerson (1803-82)
  Letters and Social Aims:
  Quotation and Originality

A fine quotation is a diamond on the finger of a man of wit, and a pebble in the hand of a fool.
- Joseph Roux (1834-86)
  Meditations of a Parish Priest

To be occasionally quoted is all the fame I care for.

- Alexander Smith (1830-67)
  Dreamthorp

RACE

After all there is but one race — humanity.
- George Moore (1852-1933)
  The Bending of the Bough,
  Act III

RACE RELATIONS

Race relations are, most probably, the most contentious field in the whole range of human culture, and it has always been so since the dawn of history.
- Jan Christian Smuts (1870-1950)
  Speech, South African Institute
  of Race Relations, Cape Town,
  South Africa, 21 January 1942

RADICAL

A radical is a man with both feet firmly planted — in the air.
- Franklin Delano Roosevelt
  (1882-1945)
  Radio Broadcast,
  26 October 1939

RAINBOW

My heart leaps up when I behold
A rainbow in the sky . . .
- William Wordsworth (1770-1850)
  My Heart Leaps Up

RANK

It is quite true, I think, that seldom, if ever, do men of low position obtain high rank except by force and by fraud, though there are, of course, others to whom rank comes merely by way of gift or inheritance. Nor do I think that force by itself ever suffices, whereas instances can easily be found in which fraud alone has sufficed.
— Niccolo Machiavelli (1469-1527)
  Discourses

REACTIONARY

A reactionary is a somnambulist walking backwards . . .
— Franklin Delano Roosevelt
  (1882-1945)
  Radio broadcast,
  26 October 1939

READING

Reading maketh a full man; conference a ready man and writing an exact man.
— Francis Bacon (1561-1626)
  Essays: Of Studies

The art of reading is to skip judiciously.
— P.G. Hamerton (1834-94)
  The Intellectual Life

Reading is sometimes an ingenious device for avoiding thought.
— Sir Arthur Helps (1813-75)
  Friends in Council

A man ought to read just as inclination leads him; for what he reads as a task will do him little good.
— Samuel Johnson (1709-84)
  Boswell's Life of Johnson

Oh! it is absurd to have a hard and fast rule about what one should read and what one shouldn't. One should read everything. More than half of modern culture depends on what one shouldn't read.
— Oscar Wilde (1854-1900)
  The Importance of Being Earnest,
  Act I

REALITY

Human kind
Cannot bear very much reality.
— T.S. Eliot (1888-1965)
  Burnt Norton

REBELS

Rebel, n. A proponent of a new misrule who has failed to establish it.
— Ambrose Bierce (1842-1914?)
  The Devil's Dictionary

What is a rebel? A man who says no.
— Albert Camus (1913-60)
  The Rebel

REBELLION

But this people hath a revolting and a rebellious heart . . .
— *Bible*, Authorized version
  Jeremiah, Ch. 5, v. 23

. . . a little rebellion, now and then, is a good thing, and as necessary in the political world as storms in the

physical.
— Thomas Jefferson (1743-1826)
  Letter to James Madison,
  30 January 1787

REFORMERS

All reformers are bachelors.
— George Moore (1852-1933)
  The Bending of the Bough, Act I

RELATIONS

Relations are simply a tedious pack
of people, who haven't got the
remotest knowledge of how to live,
nor the smallest instinct about when
to die.
— Oscar Wilde (1854-1900)
  The Importance of Being Earnest,
  Act I

RELAXATION

. . . as the bow is the stronger for
being sometimes unstrung and
unbent, so the mind will be capable
of more attention for being now and
then easy and relaxed.
— Earl of Chesterfield (1694-1773)
  Letter to his son,
  1 November 1739

RELIGION

It may be that religion is dead, and if
it is, we had better know it and set
ourselves to try to discover other
sources of moral strength before it is
too late.
— Pearl S. Buck (1892-1973)
  What America Means To Me

One religion is as true as another.
— Robert Burton (1577-1640)
  Anatomy of Melancholy

I find that the nicest and best people
generally profess no religion at all,
but are ready to like the best men of
all religions.
— Samuel Butler (1835-1902)
  Note Books

. . . a dying religion always interferes
more than it ought, not less.
— G.K. Chesterton (1874-1936)
  Daily News, 11 March 1911

Men will wrangle for religion; write
for it; fight for it; die for it; any
thing but — *live* for it.
— Reverend C.C. Colton
  (1780?-1832)
  Lacon

Many have quarrel'd about Religion,
that never practis'd it.
— Benjamin Franklin (1706-90)
  Poor Richard's Almanack, 1753

Religion without Piety hath done
more Mischief in the World, than all
other Things put together.
— Thomas Fuller (1654-1734)
  Gnomologia

Religion's in the heart, not in the
knees.
— Douglas Jerrold (1803-57)
  The Devil's Ducat, Act I

Religion is the sigh of the oppressed
creature, the feelings of a heartless
world, just as it is the spirit of
unspiritual conditions. It is the
opium of the people.
— Karl Marx (1818-83)
  Introduction to a Critique of

*the Hegelian Philosophy of
Right*

In all countries, religion is useful to
the Government; it should be used to
control the minds of the people.
– Napoleon Bonaparte (1769-1821)
  *Political Aphorisms, Moral and
  Philosophical Thoughts of the
  Emperor Napoleon*, collected by
  Cte. Ate. G. De Liancourt

Every religion is good that teaches
man to be good.
– Thomas Paine (1737-1809)
  The Rights of Man

There is only one religion, though
there are a hundred versions of it.
– George Bernard Shaw
  (1856-1950)
  Plays Pleasant and Unpleasant

We have just enough religion to make
us hate, but not enough to make us
love one another.
– Jonathan Swift (1667-1745)
  Thoughts on Various Subjects

Religions die when they are proved
to be true.
– Oscar Wilde (1854-1900)
  'Phrases and Philosophies for the
  Use of the Young', *Chameleon*,
  December, 1894

RELIGIOUS FREEDOM

Yet so natural to mankind is
intolerance in whatever they really
care about, that religious freedom has
hardly anywhere been practically
realised, except where religious
indifference, which dislikes to have
its peace disturbed by theological

quarrels, has added its weight to the
scale.
– John Stuart Mill (1806-73)
  On Liberty

REMARKABLE

Nothing is so common-place as to
wish to be remarkable.
– Oliver Wendell Holmes (1809-94)
  *The Autocrat of the Breakfast-
  Table*

REMEDIES

Some remedies are worse than the
disease.
– Publilius Syrus
  (*c.* 1st century BC)
  Maxims

REMEMBRANCE

Praising what is lost
Makes the remembrance dear.
– William Shakespeare (1564-1616)
  All's Well That Ends Well, Act V,
  Sc. III

REMINISCENCES

Reminiscences make one feel so
deliciously aged and sad.
– George Bernard Shaw
  (1856-1950)
  The Irrational Knot

REPENTANCE

Of course the sinner must repent.
But why? Simply because otherwise

he would be unable to realise what
he had done. The moment of
repentance is the moment of
initiation. More than that. It is the
means by which one alters one's past.
— Oscar Wilde (1854-1900)
De Profundis

REPETITION

Only constant repetition will finally
succeed in imprinting an idea on the
memory of the crowd.
— Adolf Hitler (1889-1945)
Mein Kampf

REPUBLICANISM

The Republican form of government
is the highest form of government;
but because of this it requires the
highest type of human nature — a
type nowhere at present existing.
— Herbert Spencer (1820-1903)
Essays: The Americans

REPUTATION

Nothing is so delicate as the
reputation of a woman; it is at once
the most beautiful and most brittle
of all human things.
— Fanny Burney (1752-1840)
Evelina

The easiest way to get a reputation is
to go outside the fold, shout around
for a few years as a violent atheist or
a dangerous radical, and then crawl
back to the shelter.
— F. Scott Fitzgerald (1896-1940)
Notebooks

Until you've lost your reputation,
you never realize what a burden it
was or what freedom really is.
— Margaret Mitchell (1900-49)
Gone with the Wind

Reputation, reputation, reputation!
O! I have lost my reputation. I have
lost the immortal part of myself,
and what remains is bestial.
— William Shakespeare (1564-1616)
Othello, Act II, Sc. III

Reputation is an idle and most false
imposition; oft got without merit,
and lost without deserving . . .
— William Shakespeare (1564-1616)
Ibid., Act II, Sc. III

RESOLUTIONS

There is a fatality about all good
resolutions. They are invariably made
too soon.
— Oscar Wilde (1854-1900)
'Phrases and Philosophies for the
Use of the Young', *Chameleon*,
December, 1894.

RESPONSIBILITY

You have only to listen to radio or
watch television for one day to gain
the firm impression that this nation,
and every section and sub-section of
it, is constantly appealing to the
Government to do this and do that,
to provide money for this and for
that, but never will you hear the view
that it is up to the individual to act.
Yet only that society is free and
remains free which burdens the
individual with responsibility.
— Walter H. Salomon (1906-   )

137

Speech, Annual General Meeting
of Rea Brothers Ltd, England,
24 April 1974

RESULTS

Results are often obtained by
Impetuosity and Daring which could
never have been obtained by
Ordinary Methods.
– Niccolo Machiavelli (1469-1527)
    Discourses

RETRACTION

Those who never retract their
opinions love themselves more than
they love truth.
– Joseph Joubert (1754-1824)
    Pensées

REVENGE

Sweet is revenge – especially to
women.
– Lord Byron (1788-1824)
    Don Juan

Revenge never repairs an Injury.
– Thomas Fuller (1654-1734)
    Gnomologia

Revenge, the longer it is delayed,
the crueller it grows.
– Thomas Fuller (1654-1734)
    Ibid.

Revenge is profitable, gratitude is
expensive.
– Edward Gibbon (1737-94)
    *Decline and Fall of the Roman
    Empire*

REVOLUTION

Revolutions are not about trifles,
but spring from trifles.
– Aristotle (384-322 BC)
    Politics

Inferiors revolt in order that they
may be equal, and equals that they
may be superior. Such is the state of
mind which creates revolutions.
– Aristotle
    Ibid.

Every revolution is the consequence
of one revolution and the beginning
of another.
– François-René de Chateaubriand
    (1768-1848)
    Revolutions Anciennes

Those who make peaceful revolution
impossible will make violent
revolution inevitable.
– John F. Kennedy (1917-63)
    Address to Latin American
    diplomats, the White House,
    12 March 1962

If by the mere force of numbers a
majority should deprive a minority of
any clearly written constitutional
right, it might, in a moral point of
view, justify revolution – certainly
would if such a right were a vital one.
– Abraham Lincoln (1809-65)
    First Inaugural Address,
    4 March 1861

Whoever sides with the revolutionary
people is a revolutionary. Whoever
sides with imperialism, feudalism and
bureaucrat-capitalism, is a counter-
revolutionary. Whoever sides with the
revolutionary people in words only
but acts otherwise is a revolutionary

in speech. Whoever sides with the revolutionary people in deed as well as in word is a revolutionary in the full sense.
— Mao Tse-tung (1893-1976)
  Speech, First National
  Committee, Chinese People's
  Political Consultative Conference,
  23 June 1950

The time to stop a revolution is at the beginning, not the end.
— Adlai Stevenson (1900-65)
  Speech, San Francisco,
  9 September 1952

The fundamental premise of a revolution is that the existing social structure has become incapable of solving the urgent problems of development of the nation.
— Leon Trotsky (1879-1940)
  History of the Russian Revolution

RICH

The rich are the scum of the earth in every country.
— G.K. Chesterton (1874-1936)
  The Flying Inn

It is only when the rich are sick, that they fully feel the impotence of wealth.
— Reverend C.C. Colton
  (1780?-1832)
  Lacon

Little Shame, little Conscience, and much Industry will make a Man rich.
— Thomas Fuller (1654-1734)
  Gnomologia

I am indeed rich, since my income is superior to my expense, and my

expense is equal to my wishes.
— Edward Gibbon (1737-94)
  Memoirs

It is better to live rich than die rich.
— Samuel Johnson (1709-84)
  Boswell's Life of Johnson

The wretchedness of being rich is that you live with rich people.
— Logan Pearsall Smith (1865-1946)
  Afterthoughts

To be thought rich is as good as to be rich.
— William Makepeace Thackeray
  (1811-63)
  The Virginians

RIDICULE

'Tis easier to ridicule than commend.
— Thomas Fuller (1654-1734)
  Gnomologia

RIDICULOUS

As there is but one step from the sublime to the ridiculous, so also there is but one from the ridiculous to the sublime.
— Samuel Butler (1835-1902)
  Note Books

RIGHT

It is wrong to be too right. To be too good is as bad — or nearly so — as to be too wicked.
— Samuel Butler (1835-1902)
  Note Books

ROGUES

Little Rogues easily become great
Ones.
— Benjamin Franklin (1706-90)
Poor Richard's Almanack, 1754

ROMANCE

Romance at short notice was her
speciality.
— Saki (H.H. Munro) (1870-1916)
*Beasts and Super-Beasts: The
Open Window*

Once a woman has given you her
heart you can never get rid of the
rest of her.
— Sir John Vanbrugh (1664-1726)
The Relapse, Act II

To love oneself is the beginning of a
lifelong romance.
— Oscar Wilde (1854-1900)
An Ideal Husband, Act III

ROYALTY

So long as the human heart is strong
and the human reason weak, Royalty
will be strong.
— Walter Bagehot (1826-77)
The English Constitution

RUIN

More have been ruined by their
servants, than by their masters.
— Reverend C.C. Colton
(1780?-1832)
Lacon

As the sutra says, a parasite in the
lion's bowels will devour the lion. A
man of great fortune cannot be
ruined by his enemies but only by
those close to him.
— Nichiren Daishonin (1222-82)
*The Major Writings of Nichiren
Daishonin: Letter from Sado*

RUMOUR

In times of calamity any rumour is
believed.
— Publilius Syrus
(*c*. 1st century BC)
Maxims

Rumour is a pipe
Blown by surmises, jealousies,
    conjectures,
And of so easy and so plain a stop
That the blunt monster with
    uncounted heads,
The still-discordant wavering
    multitude,
Can play upon it.
— William Shakespeare (1564-1616)
King Henry IV, Pt. II, Induction

SADNESS

Sadness flies away on the wings of
time.
— Jean de La Fontaine (1621-95)
La Jeune Veuve

SATIRE

Satire should, like a polished razor
    keen,
Wound with a touch that's scarcely
    felt or seen.
— Lady Mary Wortley Montagu

(1689-1762)
*To the Imitator of the First
Satire of Horace*

Satire is a sort of glass, wherein
beholders do generally discover
everybody's face but their own.
— Jonathan Swift (1667-1745)
  The Battle of the Books

SATISFACTION

It is better to be a human being
dissatisfied than a pig satisfied; better
to be a Socrates dissatisfied than a
fool satisfied.
— John Stuart Mill (1806-73)
  Utilitarianism

SCARE

A good scare is worth more to a man
than good advice.
— Edgar Watson Howe (1853-1937)
  Country Town Sayings

SCHOOLS

You can't expect a boy to be vicious
till he's been to a good school.
— Saki (H.H. Munro) (1870-1916)
  *Reginald in Russia: The Baker's
  Dozen*

SCIENCE

Man is an animal with primary
instincts of survival. Consequently,
his ingenuity has developed first and
his soul afterwards. Thus the progress
of science is far ahead of man's
ethical behaviour.

— Charlie Chaplin (1889-1977)
  My Autobiography

The whole of science is nothing more
than a refinement of everyday
thinking.
— Albert Einstein (1879-1955)
  Physics and Reality

Science is vastly more stimulating to
the imagination than are the classics.
— J.B.S. Haldane (1892-1964)
  Daedalus

Science is nothing but trained and
organized common sense, differing
from the latter only as a veteran may
differ from a raw recruit: and its
methods differ from those of
common sense only as far as the
guardsman's cut and thrust differ
from the manner in which a savage
wields his club.
— Thomas Henry Huxley (1825-95)
  *Collected Essays: The Method
  of Zadig*

Science may have found a cure for
most evils; but it has found no
remedy for the worst of them all —
the apathy of human beings.
— Helen Keller (1880-1968)
  My Religion

I almost think it is the ultimate
destiny of science to exterminate the
human race.
— Thomas Love Peacock
  (1785-1866)
  Gryll Grange

Science is organized knowledge.
— Herbert Spencer (1820-1903)
  Education

SCOTSMEN

There are few more impressive sights in the world than a Scotsman on the make.
— J.M. Barrie (1860-1937)
  What Every Woman Knows, Act I

I have been trying all my life to like Scotchmen, and am obliged to desist from the experiment in despair.
— Charles Lamb (1775-1834)
  Essays of Elia: Imperfect Sympathies

SCOUNDRELS

Every man over forty is a scoundrel.
— George Bernard Shaw (1856-1950)
  Man and Superman: Maxims for Revolutionists

SECRETS

Three may keep a Secret, if two of them are dead.
— Benjamin Franklin (1706-90)
  Poor Richard's Almanack, 1735

If you would keep your Secret from an enemy, tell it not to a friend.
— Benjamin Franklin
  Ibid., 1741

No one ever keeps a secret so well as a child.
— Victor Hugo (1802-85)
  Les Misérables

SECURITY

Most people want security in this world, not liberty.
— H.L. Mencken (1880-1956)
  Minority Report

SEEKING

What the superior man seeks is in himself. What the small man seeks is in others.
— Confucius (551-479 BC)
  Analects

SELF-CONFIDENCE

Self-confidence is the first requisite to great undertakings.
— Samuel Johnson (1709-84)
  Life of Pope

For a man who lacks self-confidence, silence is the wisest course.
— Duc de La Rochefoucauld (1613-80)
  Maxims

SELF-HELP

The spirit of self-help is the root of all genuine growth in the individual; and, exhibited in the lives of many, it constitutes the true source of national vigor and strength. Help from without is often enfeebling in its effects, but help from within invariably invigorates.
— Samuel Smiles (1812-1904)
  Self-Help

SELF INTEREST

The world will always be governed
by self interest: we should not try
and stop this: we should try and
make the self interest of cads a little
more coincident with that of decent
people.
— Samuel Butler (1835-1902)
  Note Books

SELFISHNESS

Next to the very young, I suppose
the very old are the most selfish.
— William Makepeace Thackeray
  (1811-63)
  The Virginians

SELF-PRESERVATION

Self-Preservation is Nature's first
Law.
— Thomas Fuller (1654-1734)
  Gnomologia

Self-preservation is the first law of
human nature . . .
— Jean Jacques Rousseau (1712-78)
  Du Contrat Social

SELF-SUFFICIENCY

The greatest thing in the world is to
know how to be sufficient unto
oneself.
— Michel Eyquem de Montaigne
  (1533-92)
  Essays

SENSATIONS

O for a Life of Sensations rather
than of Thoughts.
— John Keats (1795-1821)
  Letter to Benjamin Bailey,
  22 November 1817

SEX

You mustn't force sex to do the
work of love or love to do the work
of sex.
— Mary McCarthy (1912-   )
  The Group

SEXES

Instead of this absurd division into
sexes they ought to class people as
static and dynamic.
— Evelyn Waugh (1903-66)
  Decline and Fall

SEXUAL ACT

I could be content that we might
procreate like trees, without
conjunction, or that there were any
way to perpetuate the world without
this trivial and vulgar way of coition.
— Sir Thomas Browne (1605-82)
  Religio Medici

A mutual and satisfied sexual act is
of great benefit to the average
woman, the magnetism of it is health
giving.
— Margaret Sanger (1883-1966)
  Family Limitations

SHAKESPEARE

I have tried lately to read
Shakespeare, but found it so
intolerably dull that it nauseated me.
— Charles Darwin (1809-82)
Autobiography

SHAME

I never wonder to see men wicked,
but I often wonder to see them not
ashamed.
— Jonathan Swift (1667-1745)
Thoughts on Various Subjects

SHARP TONGUE

. . . a sharp tongue is the only edged
tool that grows keener with constant
use.
— Washington Irving (1783-1859)
*The Sketch Book: Rip Van
Winkle*

SHIPS

Being in a ship is being in a jail, with
the chance of being drowned.
— Samuel Johnson (1709-84)
Boswell's Life of Johnson

A ship is always referred to as a 'she'
because it costs so much to keep her
in paint.
— Admiral Chester Nimitz
(1885-1966)
New York Times, 24 May 1959

SHOCKS

Today's shocks are tomorrow's
conventions.
— Carolyn Heilbrun (1926-   )
*Toward a Recognition of
Androgyny*

SHORTCOMINGS

If we have shortcomings, we are not
afraid to have them pointed out and
criticized, because we serve the
people. Anyone, no matter who, may
point out our shortcomings. If he is
right, we will correct them. If what
he proposes will benefit the people,
we will act upon it.
— Mao Tse-tung (1893-1976)
Serve the People,
8 September 1944

SIGHS

Words may be false and full of art.
Sighs are the natural language of the
    heart.
— Thomas Shadwell (1642?-92)
Psyche, Act III

SILENCE

Silence gives consent.
— Oliver Goldsmith (1728-74)
The Good-natured Man

The silence of a friend commonly
amounts to treachery.
— William Hazlitt (1778-1830)
Characteristics

If Silence be a kind of Death,
He kindles grief who gives it breath.

– Henry King (1592-1669)
Silence

Well-timed silence hath more
eloquence than speech.
– Martin Farquhar Tupper
(1810-89)
Proverbial Philosophy

SIN

If we say that we have no sin, we
deceive ourselves, and the truth is
not in us.
– *Bible*, Authorized version
John, Ch. 1, v. 8

He that is without sin among you, let
him first cast a stone at her.
– *Bible*, Authorized version
St John, Ch. 8, v. 7

There are two classes of people in
this world, those who sin, and those
who are sinned against, if a man must
belong to either, he had better belong
to the first than to the second.
– Samuel Butler (1835-1902)
Note Books

The seven deadly sins. Want of
money, bad health, bad temper,
chastity, family ties, knowing that
you know things, and believing in
the Christian religion.
– Samuel Butler (1835-1902)
Ibid.

There is no sin except stupidity.
– Oscar Wilde (1854-1900)
The Critic as Artist

SINCERITY

Men are always sincere. They change
sincerities, that's all.
– Tristan Bernard (1866-1947)
Ce Que l'On Dit aux Femmes,
Act III

The primary condition for being
sincere is the same as for being
humble: not to boast of it, and
probably not even to be aware of it.
– Henri Peyre (1901-   )
Literature and Sincerity

A little sincerity is a dangerous thing,
and a great deal of it is absolutely
fatal.
– Oscar Wilde (1854-1900)
The Critic as Artist

SINGERS

Swans sing before they die – 'twere
no bad thing
Did certain persons die before they
sing.
– Samuel Taylor Coleridge
(1772-1834)
Epigram on a Volunteer Singer

SIZE

Therefore my proposition is 'the
larger the size, the greater the
remoteness and the greater the
remoteness the less the personal
involvement and the less the personal
involvement the smaller the profit.'
– Walter H. Salomon (1906-   )
Address, City of London Centre
of the Institute of Bankers,
30 November 1971

SLANDER

If you slander a dead Man, you stab him in the Grave.
— Thomas Fuller (1654-1734)
  Gnomologia

Done to death by slanderous tongues
. . .
— William Shakespeare (1564-1616)
  Much Ado About Nothing, Act V,
  Sc. III

SLAVERY

It is perfectly well understood at the South that to educate a slave is to make him discontented with slavery, and to invest him with a power which shall open to him the treasures of freedom . . .
— Frederick Douglass (1817-95)
  Lecture, Corinth Hall, Rochester,
  New York, 1 December 1850

SLEEP

Blessed be he who invented sleep, a cloak that covers all a man's thoughts.
— Miguel de Cervantes (1547-1616)
  Don Quixote

One Hour's sleep before Midnight, is worth two after.
— Thomas Fuller (1654-1734)
  Gnomologia

One hour's sleep before midnight is worth three after.
— George Herbert (1593-1633)
  Jacula Prudentum

SLIP OF THE TONGUE

A Slip of the Foot may be soon recover'd; but that of the Tongue perhaps never.
— Thomas Fuller (1654-1734)
  Gnomologia

SMELL

. . . a very ancient and fish-like smell
. . .
— William Shakespeare (1564-1616)
  The Tempest, Act II, Sc. II

SNEER

Who can refute a sneer?
— William Paley (1743-1805)
  *Principles of Moral and Political
  Philosophy*

SNOBBERY

It is impossible, in our condition of society, not to be sometimes a Snob.
— William Makepeace Thackeray
  (1811-63)
  The Book of Snobs

SOCIAL WORK

Social work is a band-aid on the festering wounds of society.
— Alexander Chase (1926-   )
  Perspectives

SOCIETY

Society is now one polish'd horde,
Form'd of two mighty tribes, the

Bores and *Bored*.
— Lord Byron (1788-1824)
  Don Juan

We want a society where people are
free to make choices, to make
mistakes, to be generous and
compassionate. This is what we mean
by a moral society; not a society
where the state is responsible for
everything, and no one is responsible
for the state.
— Margaret Thatcher (1925-   )
  Speech, Zurich Economic
  Society, University of Zurich,
  14 March 1977

A great society is a society in which
its men of business think greatly of
their function.
— Alfred North Whitehead
  (1861-1947)
  Adventures in Ideas

SOLDIERS

Soldiers ought more to fear their
general than their enemy.
— Michel Eyquem de Montaigne
  (1533-92)
  Essays

SOLITUDE

Whosoever is delighted in solitude is
either a wild beast or a god.
— Francis Bacon (1561-1626)
  Essays: Of Friendship

SONGS

Our sweetest songs are those which
tell of saddest thought.

— Percy Bysshe Shelley (1792-1822)
  To a Skylark

SONS

It takes a woman twenty years to
make a man of her son, and another
woman twenty minutes to make a
fool of him.
— Helen Rowland (1876-1950)
  Reflections of a Bachelor Girl

SORROW

Sorrow is tranquillity remembered
in emotion.
— Dorothy Parker (1893-1967)
  Sentiment

There are few sorrows, however
poignant, in which a good income is
of no avail.
— Logan Pearsall Smith (1865-1946)
  Afterthoughts

Pure and complete sorrow is as
impossible as pure and complete joy.
— Leo Tolstoy (1828-1910)
  War and Peace

SPEAKING

. . . he multiplieth words without
knowledge.
— *Bible*, Authorized version
  Job, Ch. 35, v. 16

Be silent, or speak something worth
hearing.
— Thomas Fuller (1654-1734)
  Gnomologia

SPECIALISTS

Woe to the specialist who is not a pretty fair generalist, and to the generalist who is not also a bit of a specialist.
- Samuel Butler (1835-1902)
  Note Books

The trouble with specialists is that they tend to think in grooves.
- Elaine Morgan (1920-   )
  The Descent of Woman

SPIRITUAL DEVELOPMENT

. . . different persons also require different conditions for their spiritual development; and can no more exist healthily in the same moral, than all the variety of plants can in the same physical, atmosphere and climate.
- John Stuart Mill (1806-73)
  On Liberty

SPRING

Nothing is so beautiful as spring . . .
- Gerard Manley Hopkins
  (1844-89)
  Spring

The cuckoo-throb, the heartbeat of the Spring . . .
- Dante Gabriel Rossetti (1828-82)
  Ardour and Memory

SQUARE DEAL

A man who is good enough to shed his blood for his country is good enough to be given a square deal afterwards. More than that no man is entitled to, and less than that no man shall have.
- Theodore Roosevelt (1858-1919)
  Speech, Springfield, Illinois,
  4 July 1903

STATE

The worth of a State, in the long run, is the worth of the individuals composing it . . .
- John Stuart Mill (1806-73)
  On Liberty

. . . a State which dwarfs its men, in order that they may be more docile instruments in its hands even for beneficial purposes — will find that with small men no great thing can really be accomplished . . .
- John Stuart Mill
  Ibid.

STATELY HOMES

Those comfortably padded lunatic asylums which are known, euphemistically, as the stately homes of England.
- Virginia Woolf (1882-1941)
  The Common Reader

STATESMEN

A constitutional statesman is in general a man of common opinions and uncommon abilities.
- Walter Bagehot (1826-77)
  Biographical Studies

STRANGER

Everyone is ready to speak evil of a stranger.
– Aeschylus (525-456 BC)
   The Suppliants

... I have been a stranger in a strange land.
– *Bible*, Authorized version
   Exodus, Ch. II, v. 22

STRENGTH

Strength lies not in defence but in attack.
– Adolf Hitler (1889-1945)
   Mein Kampf

The strongest man in the world is the man who stands alone.
– Henrik Ibsen (1828-1906)
   An Enemy of the People, Act V

The strongest is never strong enough to be always the master, unless he transforms his might into right, and obedience into duty.
– Jean Jacques Rousseau (1712-78)
   Du Contrat Social

STRIKES

There is no right to strike against the public safety by anybody, anywhere, any time.
– Calvin Coolidge (1872-1933)
   Telegram on 14 September 1919
   to Samuel Gompers (President of
   the American Federation of
   Labor) on the Boston police
   strike

STUDIES

Crafty Men contemn studies; Simple Men admire them, and Wise Men use them.
– Francis Bacon (1561-1626)
   Essays: Of Studies

... much study *is* a weariness of the flesh.
– *Bible*, Authorized version
   Ecclesiastes, Ch. 12, v. 12

It is important that students bring a certain ragamuffin, barefoot irreverence to their studies; they are not here to worship what is known, but to question it.
– Jacob Bronowski (1908-74)
   The Ascent of Man

In old days men studied for the sake of self-improvement; nowdays men study in order to impress other people.
– Confucius (551-479 BC)
   Analects

SUBJECTION

When one by force subdues men, they do not submit to him in heart. They submit because their strength is not adequate to resist.
– Mencius (372-289 BC)
   Works

SUBJECTS

There is no such thing on earth as an uninteresting subject; the only thing that can exist is an uninterested person.

Substance / Suicide

- G.K. Chesterton (1874-1936)
  Heretics

SUBSTANCE

Beware that you do not lose the
substance by grasping at the shadow.
- Aesop (*c.* 550 BC)
  Fables: The Dog and the Shadow

SUCCESS

In all things, success depends upon
previous preparation, and without
such preparation there is sure to be
failure.
- Confucius (551-479 BC)
  Analects

Success has ruin'd many a Man.
- Benjamin Franklin (1706-90)
  Poor Richard's Almanack, 1752

There are only two ways of getting
on in the world: by one's own
industry, or by the weaknesses of
others.
- Jean de La Bruyère (1645-96)
  Les Caractères

I have always observed that to
succeed in the world one should
seem a fool, but be wise.
- Baron de Montesquieu
  (1689-1755)
  Pensées Diverses

There is only one success − to be
able to spend your life in your own
way.
- Christopher Morley (1890-1957)
  Where the Blue Begins

There is a homely adage which runs,
'Speak softly and carry a big stick;
you will go far.'
- Theodore Roosevelt (1858-1919)
  Speech at Minnesota State Fair,
  2 September 1901

Success is dependent on effort.
- Sophocles (*c.* 495-406 BC)
  Electra

All you need in this life is ignorance
and confidence, and then success is
sure.
- Mark Twain (1835-1910)
  Letter to Mrs Foote,
  2 December 1878

SUFFERING

It is not true that suffering ennobles
the character; happiness does that
sometimes, but suffering, for the
most part, makes men petty and
vindictive.
- Somerset Maugham (1874-1965)
  The Moon and Sixpence

SUICIDE

Suicide sometimes proceeds from
cowardice, but not always; for
cowardice sometimes prevents it;
since as many live because they are
afraid to die, as die because they are
afraid to live.
- Reverend C.C. Colton
  (1780?-1832)
  Lacon

There is no circumstance in life
which can justify suicide.
- Napoleon Bonaparte (1769-1821)
  Political Aphorisms, Moral and

Philosophical Thoughts of the Emperor Napoleon, collected by Cte. Ate. G. De Liancourt

The relatives of a suicide always take it in bad part that he did not remain alive out of consideration for the family dignity.
— Friedrich Nietzsche (1844-1900)
  Human, All Too Human

SUNDAY

Sunday clears away the rust of the whole week.
— Joseph Addison (1672-1719)
  The Spectator, 9 July 1711

SUPERSTITION

Superstition is the religion of feeble minds.
— Edmund Burke (1729-97)
  Reflections on the Revolution in France

SURPRISE

A Man surprised is half beaten.
— Thomas Fuller (1654-1734)
  Gnomologia

TACT

Tact is after all a kind of mind-reading.
— Sarah Orne Jewett (1849-1909)
  The Country of the Pointed Firs

TALENTS

Talent is like a faucet; while it is open, one must write. Inspiration is a farce that poets have invented to give themselves importance.
— Jean Anouilh (1910-   )
  The New York Times,
  2 October 1960

All our talents increase in the using, and every faculty, both good and bad, strengthens by exercise.
— Anne Brontë (1820-49)
  The Tenant of Wildfell Hall

There is no substitute for talent. Industry and all the virtues are of no avail.
— Aldous Huxley (1894-1963)
  Point Counter Point

TALES

A tale without love is like beef without mustard: insipid.
— Anatole France (1844-1924)
  La Révolte des Anges

TALK

Men are born with *two* eyes, but with *one* tongue, in order that they should see twice as much as they say; but, from their conduct, one would suppose that they were born with two tongues, and one eye, for those talk the most who have observed the least, and obtrude their remarks upon every thing, who have seen into nothing.
— Reverend C.C. Colton
  (1780?-1832)
  Lacon

Talk / Tea

When you have nothing to say, say nothing; a weak defence strengthens your opponent, and silence is less injurious than a bad reply.
- Reverend C.C. Colton
  Ibid.

Words learn'd by rote a parrot may rehearse,
But talking is not always to converse
  . . .
- William Cowper (1731-1800)
  Conversation

He that speaks much, is much mistaken.
- Benjamin Franklin (1706-90)
  Poor Richard's Almanack, 1736

TALKERS

Great Talkers, little Doers.
- Benjamin Franklin (1706-90)
  Poor Richard's Almanack, 1733

The eternal Talker neither hears nor learns.
- Thomas Fuller (1654-1734)
  Gnomologia

Talkers are no good doers . . .
- William Shakespeare (1564-1616)
  King Richard III, Act I, Sc. III

TASTE

Every one carries his own inch-rule of taste, and amuses himself by applying it, triumphantly, wherever he travels.
- Henry Brooks Adams
  (1838-1918)
  The Education of Henry Adams

People care more about being thought to have taste than about being thought either good, clever, or amiable.
- Samuel Butler (1835-1902)
  Note Books

TAUNTS

So long as I am acting from duty and conviction, I am indifferent to taunts and jeers. I think they will probably do me more good than harm.
- Sir Winston Churchill
  (1874-1965)
  Speech, House of Commons,
  6 December 1945

TAXES

Taxes, after all, are the dues that we pay for the privileges of membership in an organized society.
- Franklin Delano Roosevelt
  (1882-1945)
  Speech, Worcester, Massachusetts,
  21 October 1936

The more living standards are squeezed by taxation, the greater is the temptation to evade that taxation.
- Margaret Thatcher (1925-   )
  Speech, Zurich Economic
  Society, University of Zurich,
  14 March 1977

TEA

It has been well said that tea is suggestive of a thousand wants, from which spring the decencies and luxuries of civilization.

– Agnes Repplier (1858-1950)
  To Think of Tea!

TEACHERS

A teacher affects eternity; he can
never tell where his influence stops.
– Henry Brooks Adams
  (1838-1918)
  The Education of Henry Adams

He who can, does. He who cannot,
teaches.
– George Bernard Shaw
  (1856-1950)
  *Man and Superman: Maxims
  for Revolutionists*

Everybody who is incapable of
learning has taken to teaching.
– Oscar Wilde (1854-1900)
  The Decay of Lying

TEMPER

Never lose your temper with the
Press or the public is a major rule
of political life.
– Christabel Pankhurst (1880-1958)
  Unshackled

TEMPTATION

I never resist temptation, because I
have found that things that are bad
for me do not tempt me.
– George Bernard Shaw
  (1856-1950)
  The Apple Cart, Act II

I couldn't help it. I can resist
everything except temptation.

– Oscar Wilde (1854-1900)
  Lady Windermere's Fan, Act I

The only way to get rid of a
temptation is to yield to it.
– Oscar Wilde (1854-1900)
  The Picture of Dorian Gray

THEATRE

It's one of the tragic ironies of the
theatre that only one man in it can
count on steady work – the night
watchman.
– Tallulah Bankhead (1903-68)
  Tallulah

THEOLOGY

Theology is an attempt to explain a
subject by men who do not
understand it. The intent is not to
tell the truth but to satisfy the
questioner.
– Elbert Hubbard (1856-1915)
  The Philistines

THEORIES

Very dangerous things, theories.
– Dorothy L. Sayers (1893-1957)
  *The Unpleasantness at the Bellona
  Club*

THEORIZE

It is a capital mistake to theorize
before one has data.
– Sir Arthur Conan Doyle
  (1859-1930)
  Scandal in Bohemia

THINKING

To most people nothing is more
troublesome than the effort of
thinking.
- James Bryce (1838-1922)
  *Studies in History and
  Jurisprudence*

We think as we do, mainly because
other people think so.
- Samuel Butler (1835-1902)
  Note Books

When he was expected to use his
mind, he felt like a right-handed
person who has to do something with
his left hand.
- Georg Christoph Lichtenberg
  (1742-99)
  Aphorisms

If you make people think they're
thinking, they'll love you. If you
really make them think, they'll hate
you.
- Don Marquis (1878-1937)
  The Sun Dial

THOUGHTS

I prefer thought to action, an idea to
an event, reflection to activity.
- Honoré de Balzac (1799-1850)
  Louis Lambert

First thoughts are best, being those
of generous impulse; whereas Second
Thoughts are those of Selfish
Prudence.
- Edward FitzGerald (1809-83)
  Polonius: Second Thoughts

A thought is often original, though
you have uttered it a hundred times.

- Oliver Wendell Holmes (1809-94)
  *The Autocrat of the Breakfast
  Table*

When a thought is too weak to be
expressed simply, it is a proof that it
should be rejected.
- Luc de Clapiers, Marquis de
  Vauvenargues (1715-47)
  Réflexions et Maximes

TIME

To every *thing there is* a season, and
a time to every purpose under the
heaven: A time to be born, and a
time to die . . .
- *Bible*, Authorized version
  Ecclesiastes, Ch. 3, vs 1 and 2

Lost Time is never found again.
- Benjamin Franklin (1706-90)
  Poor Richard's Almanack, 1748

You may delay, but *Time* will not.
- Benjamin Franklin,
  Ibid., 1758

All things decay with Time.
- Robert Herrick (1591-1674)
  *Hesperides: All Things Decay and
  Die*

Time – the devourer of all things.
- Ovid (43 BC-17 AD)
  Metamorphoses

Time: that which man is always
trying to kill, but which ends in
killing him.
- Herbert Spencer (1820-1903)
  Definitions

TOBACCO

A custom loathesome to the eye,
hateful to the nose, harmful to the
brain, dangerous to the lungs, and in
the black, stinking fume thereof,
nearest resembling the horrible
Stygian smoke of the pit that is
bottomless.
— King James I of England and
  VI of Scotland (1566-1625)
  A Counterblast to Tobacco

TORY

He thinks like a Tory, and talks like
a Radical, and that's so important
nowadays.
— Oscar Wilde (1854-1900)
  Lady Windermere's Fan, Act II

TRADITION

Tradition is a guide and not a jailer.
— Somerset Maugham (1874-1965)
  The Summing Up

TRAGEDY

We participate in a tragedy; at a
comedy we only look.
— Aldous Huxley (1894-1963)
  The Devils of Loudun

TRAINING

Train up a child in the way he should
go: and when he is old, he will not
depart from it.
— *Bible*, Authorized version
  Proverbs, Ch. 22, v. 6

Training is everything. The peach was
once a bitter almond; cauliflower
is nothing but cabbage with a college
education.
— Mark Twain (1835-1910)
  Pudd'nhead Wilson's Calendar

TRANQUILLITY

A man who cannot find tranquillity
within himself will search for it in
vain elsewhere.
— Duc de La Rochefoucauld
  (1613-80)
  Maxims

TRAVEL

Travel, in the younger sort, is a part
of education; in the elder, a part of
experience.
— Francis Bacon (1561-1626)
  Essays: Of Travel

He that would travel much, should
eat little.
— Benjamin Franklin (1706-90)
  Poor Richard's Almanack, 1755

He that travels much, knows much.
— Thomas Fuller (1654-1734)
  Gnomologia

I should like to spend the whole of
my life in travelling abroad, if I could
anywhere borrow another life to
spend afterwards at home.
— William Hazlitt (1778-1830)
  On Going a Journey

TREASURE

No treasure possessed by man is more
precious than food and drink,
clothing and medicine.
- Nichiren Daishonin (1222-82)
  *The Major Writings of Nichiren
  Daishonin: General Stone Tiger*

TREATIES

Treaties are like roses and young
girls. They last while they last.
- Charles de Gaulle (1890-1970)
  Time, 12 July 1963

TREES

I like trees because they seem more
resigned to the way they have to live
than other things do.
- Willa Cather (1873-1947)
  O Pioneers!

TRUST

Men trust their ears less than their
eyes.
- Herodotus (*c*. 485-*c*. 425 BC)
  The Histories of Herodotus

It is better never to trust anybody.
- Henrik Ibsen (1828-1906)
  An Enemy of the People

He who does not trust enough will
not be trusted.
- Lao-tzu (*c*. 604-*c*. 531 BC)
  Tao Te Ching

TRUTH

Truth exists, only falsehood has to
be invented.
- Georges Braque (1882-1963)
  Pensées sur l'Art

Truth is like the use of words, it
depends greatly upon custom.
- Samuel Butler (1835-1902)
  Note Books

It is not so difficult a task to plant
new truths, as to root out old errors;
for there is this paradox in men, they
run after that which is new, but are
prejudiced in favour of that which is
old.
- Reverend C.C. Colton
  (1780?-1832)
  Lacon

It is an old maxim of mine that when
you have excluded the impossible,
whatever remains, however
improbable, must be the truth.
- Sir Arthur Conan Doyle
  (1859-1930)
  The Beryl Coronet

Truth is immortal; error is mortal.
- Mary Baker Eddy (1821-1910)
  *Science and Health, with Key to
  the Scriptures*

Children and Fools tell the Truth.
- Thomas Fuller (1654-1734)
  Gnomologia

Truth never damages a cause that is
just.
- Mahatma Gandhi (1869-1948)
  Non-Violence in Peace and War

It is the customary fate of new truths
to begin as heresies and to end as

superstitions.
- Thomas Henry Huxley (1825-95)
  Science and Culture

It is one thing to show a man that he is in error, and another to put him in possession of truth.
- John Locke (1632-1704)
  Essay Concerning Human Understanding

Truth, in the great practical concerns of life, is so much a question of the reconciling and combining of opposites, that very few have minds sufficiently capacious and impartial to make the adjustment with an approach to correctness, and it has to be made by the rough process of a struggle between combatants fighting under hostile banners.
- John Stuart Mill (1806-73)
  On Liberty

Truth gains more even by the errors of one who, with due study and preparation, thinks for himself, than by the true opinions of those who only hold them because they do not suffer themselves to think.
- John Stuart Mill
  Ibid.

No human being is constituted to know the truth, the whole truth and nothing but the truth; and even the best of men must be content with fragments, with partial glimpses, never the full fruition.
- Sir William Osler (1849-1919)
  The Student Life

Truth often suffers more by the heat of its defenders than from the arguments of its opposers.
- William Penn (1644-1718)

Some Fruits of Solitude, in Reflections and Maxims relating to the Conduct of Human Life

. . . in the end truth will out.
- William Shakespeare (1564-1616)
  The Merchant of Venice, Act II, Sc. II

All great truths begin as blasphemies.
- George Bernard Shaw (1856-1950)
  Annajanska

There was things which he stretched, but mainly he told the truth.
- Mark Twain (1835-1910)
  The Adventures of Huckleberry Finn

The truth is rarely pure, and never simple.
- Oscar Wilde (1854-1900)
  The Importance of Being Earnest, Act I

If one tells the truth, one is sure, sooner or later, to be found out.
- Oscar Wilde (1854-1900)
  'Phrases and Philosophies for the Use of the Young', *Chameleon*, December, 1894

If you shut up truth and bury it under the ground, it will but grow, and gather to itself such explosive power that the day it bursts through it will blow up everything in its way.
- Émile Zola (1840-1902)
  J'accuse

TYRANTS

Kings will be tyrants from policy, when subjects are rebels from

principle.
- Edmund Burke (1729-97)
  *Reflections on the Revolution
  in France*

UNCERTAINTY

Uncertainty is painful for all people,
and for all men.
- Napoleon Bonaparte (1769-1821)
  *Political Aphorisms, Moral and
  Philosophical Thoughts of the
  Emperor Napoleon*, collected by
  Cte. Ate. G. De Liancourt

UNDERSTANDING

It is better to understand little than
to misunderstand a lot.
- Anatole France (1844-1924)
  Revolt of the Angels

UNDERTAKERS

It is a disturbing truth that even
undertakers die sometimes.
- Arnold Bennett (1867-1931)
  In a New Bottle

UNITY

The unification of our country, the
unity of our people and the unity of
our various nationalities — these are
the basic guarantees of the sure
triumph of our cause.
- Mao Tse-tung (1893-1976)
  *On the Correct Handling of
  Contradictions Among the
  People*, 27 February 1957

UNIVERSITIES

Universities incline wits to sophistry
and affectation.
- Francis Bacon (1561-1626)
  *Valerius Terminus of the
  Interpretation of Nature*

The true University of these days is a
collection of books.
- Thomas Carlyle (1795-1881)
  Heroes and Hero-Worship

A university should be a place of
light, of liberty, and of learning.
- Benjamin Disraeli (1804-81)
  Speech, House of Commons,
  11 March 1873

UPPER CLASSES

One has often wondered whether
upon the whole earth there is
anything so unintelligent, so unapt to
perceive how the world is really
going, as an ordinary young
Englishman of our upper classes.
- Matthew Arnold (1822-88)
  Culture and Anarchy

UTILITARIANISM

The creed which accepts as the
foundation of morals, Utility, or the
Greatest Happiness Principle, holds
that actions are right in proportion as
they tend to promote happiness,
wrong as they tend to produce the
reverse of happiness.
- John Stuart Mill (1806-73)
  Utilitarianism

VALOUR

The better part of valour is
indiscretion.
– Samuel Butler (1835-1902)
  Note Books

VANITY

Vanity plays lurid tricks with our
memory.
– Joseph Conrad (1857-1924)
  Lord Jim

VARIETY

Variety is the soul of pleasure.
– Aphra Behn (1640-89)
  The Rover

Variety is the mother of enjoyment.
– Benjamin Disraeli (1804-81)
  Vivian Grey

No pleasure lasts long unless there is
variety in it.
– Publilius Syrus
  (*c.* 1st century BC)
  Maxims

VENGEANCE

Delay in vengeance gives a heavier
blow.
– John Ford (*c.* 1586-1639)
  'Tis a Pity She's a Whore, Act IV

VICE

The second Vice is Lying; the first is
Running in Debt.

– Benjamin Franklin (1706-90)
  Poor Richard's Almanack, 1748

I prefer an accommodating vice to an
obstinate virtue.
– Molière (1622-73)
  Amphitryon

The vice which offends no one is not
really vice.
– Michel Eyquem de Montaigne
  (1533-92)
  Essays

What were once vices are now the
manners of the day.
– Seneca (*c.* 4 BC-65 AD)
  Ad Lucilium

VICTORY

Victory at all costs, victory in spite
of all terror, victory however long
and hard the road may be; for
without victory there is no survival.
– Sir Winston Churchill
  (1874-1965)
  Speech, House of Commons,
  13 May 1940

A victory without danger is a
triumph without glory.
– Pierre Corneille (1606-84)
  Le Cid

The one means that wins the easiest
victory over reason: terror and force.
– Adolf Hitler (1889-1945)
  Mein Kampf

VIEWS

Time and circumstance, which
enlarge the views of most men,

narrow the views of women almost invariably.
- Thomas Hardy (1840-1928)
  Jude the Obscure

VILLAINS

. . . one may smile, and smile, and be a villain.
- William Shakespeare (1564-1616)
  Hamlet, Act I, Sc. V

VIRGIN

Who dies a virgin lives a saint on earth.
- John Ford (*c.* 1586-1639)
  'Tis a Pity She's a Whore, Act IV

VIRTUE

Virtue, perhaps, is nothing more than politeness of soul.
- Honoré de Balzac (1799-1850)
  The Physiology of Marriage

There is no road or ready way to virtue.
- Sir Thomas Browne (1605-82)
  Religio Medici

The only reward of virtue is virtue; the only way to have a friend is to be one.
- Ralph Waldo Emerson (1803-82)
  Essays: Friendship

Genuine Virtue counts in Difficult Times, but, when Things are going well, it is rather to those whose Popularity is due to Wealth or Parentage that Men look.
- Niccolo Machiavelli

(1469-1527)
Discourses

When we are planning for posterity, we ought to remember that virtue is not hereditary.
- Thomas Paine (1737-1809)
  Common Sense

Virtue consists, not in abstaining from vice, but in not desiring it.
- George Bernard Shaw
  (1856-1950)
  Man and Superman: Maxims for Revolutionists

VIRTUOUS

The more virtuous any man is, the less easily does he suspect others to be vicious.
- Cicero (106-43 BC)
  Ad Fratrem

VISION

Where *there is* no vision, the people perish . . .
- *Bible*, Authorized version
  Proverbs, Ch. 29, v. 18

VOTING

I always voted at my party's call,
And I never thought of thinking for
    myself at all.
- W.S. Gilbert (1836-1911)
  HMS Pinafore

WAR

In peace the sons bury their fathers
and in war the fathers bury their sons.
— Francis Bacon (1561-1626)
  Apothegms

It is not merely cruelty that leads
men to love war, it is excitement.
— Henry Ward Beecher (1813-87)
  Proverbs from Plymouth Pulpit

In war, whichever side may call itself
the victor, there are no winners, but
all are losers.
— Neville Chamberlain (1869-1940)
  Speech, Kettering, England,
  3 July 1938

When the British people make up
their minds to go to war they expect
to receive terrible injuries. That is
why we tried to remain at peace as
long as possible.
— Sir Winston Churchill
  (1874-1965)
  Speech, House of Commons,
  5 September 1940

A wise minister would rather preserve
peace, than gain a victory; because he
knows that, even the most successful
war leaves nations generally more
poor, always more profligate than it
found them.
— Reverend C.C. Colton
  (1780?-1832)
  Lacon

All delays are dangerous in war.
— John Dryden (1631-1700)
  Tyrannic Love, Act I

Frankly, I'd like to see the
government get out of war altogether
and leave the whole field to private
industry.
— Joseph Heller (1923-)
  Catch-22

They wrote in the old days that it is
sweet and fitting to die for one's
country. But in modern war there is
nothing sweet nor fitting in your
dying. You will die like a dog for no
good reason.
— Ernest Hemingway (1898-1961)
  Notes on the Next War

In war there is no substitute for
victory.
— Douglas MacArthur (1880-1964)
  Address to a Joint Meeting of
  Congress, 19 April 1951

We are advocates of the abolition of
war, we do not want war; but war
can only be abolished through war,
and in order to get rid of the gun it is
necessary to take up the gun.
— Mao Tse-tung (1893-1976)
  Problems of War and Strategy,
  6 November 1938

Weapons are an important factor in
war, but not the decisive factor; it is
people, not things, that are decisive.
The contest of strength is not only a
contest of military and economic
power, but also a contest of human
power and morale.
— Mao Tse-tung (1893-1976)
  On Protracted War, May, 1938

War alone keys up all human energies
to their maximum tension and sets
the seal of nobility on those people
who have the courage to face it.
— Benito Mussolini (1883-1945)
  Fascism

War / Well-Bred

When the rich make war, it's the poor
who die.
— Jean-Paul Sartre (1905-80)
   Le Diable et le Bon Dieu

The first and most imperative
necessity in war is money, for money
means everything else — men, guns,
ammunition.
— Ida Tarbell (1857-1944)
   The Tariff in Our Times

As long as war is regarded as wicked,
it will always have its fascination.
When it is looked upon as vulgar, it
will cease to be popular. The change
will, of course, be slow, and people
will not be conscious of it.
— Oscar Wilde (1854-1900)
   The Critic as Artist

WASTE

In my creed, waste of public money
is like the sin against the Holy Ghost.
— Lord Morley (Viscount Morley of
   Blackburn) (1838-1923)
   Recollections

WEALTH

Wealth maketh many friends . . .
— *Bible*, Authorized version
   Proverbs, Ch. 19, v. 4

Surplus wealth is a sacred trust which
its possessor is bound to administer
in his lifetime for the good of the
community.
— Andrew Carnegie (1835-1919)
   The Gospel of Wealth

Wealth is not his that has it, but his
that enjoys it.

— Benjamin Franklin (1706-90)
   Poor Richard's Almanack, 1736

He who multiplies Riches multiplies
Cares.
— Benjamin Franklin
   Ibid., 1744

A good Wife & Health, is a Man's
best Wealth.
— Benjamin Franklin
   Ibid., 1746

Wealth and Content are not always
Bed-fellows.
— Benjamin Franklin
   Ibid., 1749

Great Wealth makes us neither more
Wise, nor more Healthy.
— Thomas Fuller (1654-1734)
   Gnomologia

There is no road to wealth so easy
and respectable as that of matrimony.
— Anthony Trollope (1815-82)
   Doctor Thorne

WELL-BRED

The characteristic of a well-bred man
is, to converse with his inferiors
without insolence, and with his
superiors with respect and ease.
— Earl of Chesterfield (1694-1773)
   Letter to his son, 17 May 1748

He is not well-bred, that cannot bear
Ill-Breeding in others.
— Benjamin Franklin (1706-90)
   Poor Richard's Almanack, 1748

WELSH

'The Welsh,' said the Doctor, 'are the
only nation in the world that has
produced no graphic or plastic art,
no architecture, no drama. They just
sing,' he said with disgust, 'sing and
blow down wind instruments of
plated silver.'
— Evelyn Waugh (1903-66)
  Decline and Fall

WICKEDNESS

Wickedness is a myth invented by
good people to account for the
curious attractiveness of others.
— Oscar Wilde (1854-1900)
  'Phrases and Philosophies for the
  Use of the Young', *Chameleon*,
  December, 1894

WIFE

wife. It is used for a woman of low
employment.
— Samuel Johnson (1709-84)
  Dictionary

WILL

Men may be convinced, but they
cannot be pleased, against their will.
— Samuel Johnson (1709-84)
  Life of Congreve

WINTER

. . . winter tames man, woman, and
beast.
— William Shakespeare (1564-1616)

The Taming of the Shrew,
Act IV, Sc. I

WISDOM

A man may learn wisdom even from
a foe.
— Aristophanes (*c*. 444-380 BC)
  The Birds

For in much wisdom *is* much grief:
and he that increaseth knowledge
increaseth sorrow.
— *Bible*, Authorized version
  Ecclesiastes, Ch. 1, v. 18

For wisdom *is* better than rubies;
and all the things that may be desired
are not to be compared to it.
— *Bible*, Authorized version
  Proverbs, Ch. 8, v. 11

Be wiser than other people if you
can: but do not tell them so.
— Earl of Chesterfield (1694-1773)
  Letter to his son,
  19 November 1745

Wit and Wisdom are like the seven
Stars: seldom seen together.
— Thomas Fuller (1654-1734)
  Gnomologia

The only medicine for suffering,
crime, and all the other woes of
mankind, is wisdom.
— Thomas Henry Huxley (1825-95)
  Science and Education

From the earliest times the old have
rubbed it into the young that they
are wiser than they, and before the
young had discovered what nonsense
this was they were old too, and it
profited them to carry on the

163

imposture.
- Somerset Maugham (1874-1965)
  Cakes and Ale

Some folk are wise, and some are otherwise.
- Tobias Smollett (1721-71)
  Roderick Random

Sciences may be learned by rote, but Wisdom not.
- Laurence Sterne (1713-68)
  Tristram Shandy

WIT

For when the wine is in, the wit is out.
- Thomas Becon (1512-67)
  Catechism

. . . reputation is a spur to wit,
And some wits flag through fear of losing it.
- William Cowper (1731-1800)
  Table Talk

True wit is nature to advantage dressed,
What oft was thought, but ne'er so well expressed.
- Alexander Pope (1688-1744)
  An Essay on Criticism

. . . brevity is the soul of wit.
- William Shakespeare (1564-1616)
  Hamlet, Act II, Sc. II

WIVES

Wives are young men's mistresses, companions for middle age, and old men's nurses.
- Francis Bacon (1561-1626)

  Essays: Of Marriage and Single Life

A virtuous woman *is* a crown to her husband . . .
- *Bible*, Authorized version
  Proverbs, Ch. 12, v. 4

Whoso findeth a wife findeth a good *thing*, and obtaineth favour of the LORD.
- *Bible*, Authorized version
  Ibid., Ch. 18, v. 22

He that has not got a Wife, is not yet a compleat Man.
- Benjamin Franklin (1706-90)
  Poor Richard's Almanack, 1744

A Man's best Fortune, or his worst, is a Wife.
- Thomas Fuller (1654-1734)
  Gnomologia

A Wife is not to be chosen by the Eye only.
- Thomas Fuller (1654-1734)
  Ibid.

One wife is too much for most husbands to hear
But two at a time there's no mortal can bear.
- John Gay (1685-1732)
  The Beggar's Opera

I . . . chose my wife, as she did her wedding gown, not for a fine glossy surface, but such qualities as would wear well.
- Oliver Goldsmith (1728-74)
  The Vicar of Wakefield

Suspicion, Discontent, and Strife, Come in for Dowrie with a Wife.
- Robert Herrick (1591-1674)

*Hesperides: Single Life Most
Secure*

There is no greater misfortune for a
man than to be governed by his wife:
in such case he is neither himself nor
his wife, he is a perfect nonentity.
- Napoleon Bonaparte (1769-1821)
  *Political Aphorisms, Moral and
  Philosophical Thoughts of the
  Emperor Napoleon*, collected by
  Cte. Ate. G. De Liancourt

One man's folly is another man's
wife.
- Helen Rowland (1876-1950)
  Reflections of a Bachelor Girl

An ideal wife is any woman who has
an ideal husband.
- Booth Tarkington (1869-1946)
  *Looking Forward to the Great
  Adventure*

There are no wives like English wives,
So fair and chaste as they be.
- Alfred, Lord Tennyson (1809-92)
  National Song

A wife's faults must either be put
down or put up with.
- Varro (116-27 BC)
  Menippean Satires

WOMEN

A woman can be anything that the
man who loves her would have her be.
- J.M. Barrie (1860-1937)
  Tommy and Grizel

Most women are not so young as
they are painted.
- Sir Max Beerbohm (1872-1956)
  A Defence of Cosmetics

And the rib, which the LORD God
had taken from man, made he a
woman . . .
- *Bible*, Authorized version
  Genesis, Ch. 2, v. 22

Woman would be more charming if
one could fall into her arms without
falling into her hands.
- Ambrose Bierce (1842-1914?)
  Epigrams

What is bettre than wisdom?
Womman. And what is bettre than a
good womman? No-thing.
- Geoffrey Chaucer (1340?-1400)
  *The Canterbury Tales: Tale of
  Melibee*

Women, then, are only children of a
larger growth; they have an
entertaining tattle and sometimes
wit; but for solid reasoning and good-
sense, I never in my life knew one
that had it, or who reasoned and
acted consequentially for four-and-
twenty hours together.
- Earl of Chesterfield (1694-1773)
  Letter to his son,
  5 September 1748

Women are much more like each
other than men; they have, in truth,
but two passions, vanity and love;
these are their universal
characteristics.
- Earl of Chesterfield
  Ibid., 19 December 1749

Women and people of low birth are
very hard to deal with. If you are
friendly with them, they get out of
hand, and if you keep your distance,
they resent it.
- Confucius (551-479 BC)
  Analects

Women

Heav'n has no rage, like love to
　　hatred turn'd,
Nor Hell a fury, like a woman scorn'd.
— William Congreve (1670-1729)
　　The Mourning Bride, Act III

But what is woman? — only one of
Nature's agreeable blunders.
— Hannah Cowley (1743-1809)
　　Who's The Dupe? Act II

I'm not denyin' the women are
foolish: God Almighty made 'em to
match the men.
— George Eliot (1819-80)
　　Adam Bede

The happiest women, like the
happiest nations, have no history.
— George Eliot (1819-80)
　　The Mill on the Floss

I should like to know what is the
proper function of women, if it is
not to make reasons for husbands to
stay at home, and still stronger
reasons for bachelors to go out.
— George Eliot
　　Ibid.

Women and music should never be
dated.
— Oliver Goldsmith (1728-74)
　　She Stoops to Conquer, Act III

Women have often more of what is
called good sense than men. They
have fewer pretensions; are less
implicated in theories; and judge of
objects more from their immediate
and involuntary impression on the
mind, and, therefore, more truly and
naturally. They cannot reason wrong;
for they do not reason at all.
— William Hazlitt (1778-1830)
　　The Ignorance of the Learned

A woman's mind is cleaner than a
man's — she changes it oftener.
— Oliver Herford (1863-1935)
　　Epigram

For the female of the species is more
deadly than the male.
— Rudyard Kipling (1865-1936)
　　The Female of the Species

Women run to extremes; they are
either better or worse than men.
— Jean de La Bruyère (1645-96)
　　Les Caractères

I expect that Woman will be the last
thing civilized by Man.
— George Meredith (1828-1909)
　　The Ordeal of Richard Feverel

Woman was God's second blunder.
— Friedrich Nietzsche (1844-1900)
　　The Antichrist

In revenge and in love woman is more
barbarous than man.
— Friedrich Nietzsche (1844-1900)
　　Beyond Good and Evil

She wavers, she hesitates; in a word,
she is a woman.
— Jean Racine (1639-99)
　　Athalie, Act III

A woman is like a tea-bag. It's only
when she's in hot water that you
realise how strong she is.
— Nancy Reagan (1921-　　)
　　quoted in *Daily Mail*, 27 March
　　1981 but used as a comment by
　　her prior to that date

But I don't believe women ever get
sensible, not even through prolonged
association with their husbands.
— Dorothy L. Sayers (1893-1957)

*The Unpleasantness at the
Bellona Club*

Do you not know I am a woman?
when I think, I must speak.
— William Shakespeare (1564-1616)
   As You Like It, Act III, Sc. II

Women are wiser than men because
they know less and understand more.
— James Stephens (1882-1950)
   The Crock of Gold

Women never look so well as when
one comes in wet and dirty from
hunting.
— R.S. Surtees (1803-64)
   Mr Sponge's Sporting Tour

Woman is the lesser man.
— Alfred, Lord Tennyson (1809-92)
   Locksley Hall

Woman is always a variable and
changeable thing.
— Virgil (70-19 BC)
   Aeneid

All women become like their mothers.
That is their tragedy. No man does.
That's his.
— Oscar Wilde (1854-1900)
   The Importance of Being Earnest,
   Act I

One should never trust a woman who
tells one her real age. A woman who
would tell one that, would tell one
anything.
— Oscar Wilde (1854-1900)
   A Woman of No Importance,
   Act I

WOMEN'S RIGHTS

The extension of women's rights is
the basic principle of all social
progress.
— Charles Fourier (1772-1837)
   Théorie des Quatre Mouvements

WORDS

Words may shew a man's Wit, but
Actions his Meaning.
— Benjamin Franklin (1706-90)
   Poor Richard's Almanack, 1749

An acute Word cuts deeper than a
sharp Weapon.
— Thomas Fuller (1654-1734)
   Gnomologia

Good words cost nothing, but are
worth much.
— Thomas Fuller
   Ibid.

Good Words cost no more than bad.
— Thomas Fuller
   Ibid.

Those who have much leisure to
think, will always be enlarging the
stock of ideas, and every increase of
knowledge, whether real or fancied,
will produce new words, or
combinations of words.
— Samuel Johnson (1709-84)
   Dictionary

We should have a great many fewer
disputes in the world if words were
taken for what they are, the signs of
our ideas only, and not for things
themselves.
— John Locke (1632-1704)

Words / Work

Essay Concerning Human Understanding

Words are like leaves; and where
  they most abound,
Much fruit of sense beneath is rarely
  found.
— Alexander Pope (1688-1744)
  Essay on Criticism

WORK

What is worth doing is worth the
trouble of asking somebody to do it.
— Ambrose Bierce (1842-1914?)
  The Devil's Dictionary

A man's work whether in music,
painting or literature is always a
portrait of himself.
— Samuel Butler (1835-1902)
  Note Books

The only living works are those
which have drained much of the
author's own life into them.
— Samuel Butler
  Ibid.

Work is the grand cure of all the
maladies and miseries that ever
beset mankind.
— Thomas Carlyle (1795-1881)
  Rectorial Address, Edinburgh,
  2 April 1866

'A fair day's wages for a fair day's
work': it is as just a demand as
governed men ever made of
governing. It is the everlasting right
of man.
— Thomas Carlyle (1795-1881)
  Past and Present

There is no one thing so trifling, but
which (if it is to be done at all)
ought to be done well.
— Earl of Chesterfield (1694-1773)
  Letter to his son,
  19 November 1745

Mortals live by work and wages.
— Friedrich Hölderlin (1770-1843)
  Abendphantasie

Life grants nothing to us mortals
without hard work.
— Horace (65-8 BC)
  Satires

I like work: it fascinates me. I can sit
and look at it for hours.
— Jerome K. Jerome (1859-1927)
  Three Men in a Boat

Works expands so as to fill the time
available for its completion.
— C. Northcote Parkinson (1909-)
  Parkinson's Law

Work is accomplished by those
employees who have not yet reached
their level of incompetence.
— Laurence Peter (1919-)
  The Peter Principle

In order that people may be happy in
their work, these three things are
needed: They must be fit for it: They
must not do too much of it: And
they must have a sense of success in
it.
— John Ruskin (1819-1900)
  Pre-Raphaelitism

Work keeps us from three great evils,
boredom, vice, and need.
— Voltaire (1694-1778)
  Candide

WORLD

All the world's a stage
And all the men and women merely
    players.
— William Shakespeare (1564-1616)
    As You Like It, Act II, Sc. VII

WORLD POLICY

In the field of world policy I would
dedicate this nation to the policy
of the good neighbour.
— Franklin Delano Roosevelt
    (1882-1945)
    First Inaugural Address,
    4 March 1933

WORRY

He who will not worry about what is
far off will soon find something
worse than worry close at hand.
— Confucius (551-479 BC)
    Analects

WORTH

A thing is worth whatever the buyer
will pay for it.
— Publilius Syrus
    (*c*. 1st century BC)
    Maxims

WRITERS

Writers, like teeth, are divided into
incisors and grinders.
— Walter Bagehot (1826-77)
    *Estimates of some Englishmen
    and Scotchmen*

That writer does the most, who gives
his reader the *most* knowledge, and
takes from him the *least* time.
— Reverend C.C. Colton
    (1780?-1832)
    Lacon

If you wish to be a writer, write.
— Epictetus (*c*. 50-*c*. 120)
    Discourses

As writers become more numerous, it
is natural for readers to become more
indolent.
— Oliver Goldsmith (1728-74)
    The Bee

WRITING

True ease in writing comes from art,
not chance.
— Alexander Pope (1688-1744)
    An Essay on Criticism

Writing, when properly managed (as
you may be sure I think mine is), is
but a different name for conversation.
— Laurence Sterne (1713-68)
    Tristram Shandy

Three hours a day will produce as
much as a man ought to write.
— Anthony Trollope (1815-82)
    Autobiography

WRONG

A man should never be ashamed to
own he has been in the wrong, which
is but saying, in other words, that he
is wiser today than he was yesterday.
— Jonathan Swift (1667-1745)
    Thoughts on Various Subjects

YOUNG PEOPLE

The young people are the most active and vital force in society. They are the most eager to learn and the least conservative in their thinking.
— Mao Tse-tung (1893-1976)
  The Socialist Upsurge in China's Countryside

YOUTH

Youth is like spring, an overpraised season.
— Samuel Butler (1835-1902)
  The Way of All Flesh

Almost everything that is great has been done by youth.
— Benjamin Disraeli (1804-81)
  Coningsby

Youth is a blunder; Manhood a struggle; Old Age a regret.
— Benjamin Disraeli
  Ibid.

We cannot always build the future for our youth, but we can build our youth for the future.
— Franklin Delano Roosevelt (1882-1945)
  Speech, University of Pennsylvania, Philadelphia, USA, 20 September 1940

INDEX OF AUTHORS

Index of Authors

Scotsmen, Women

Auguste Barthélemy (1796-1867):
Change

Charles Baudelaire (1821-67): Art

Vicki Baum (1888-1960): Marriage

Pierre Bayle (1647-1706):
Christianity

Francis Beaumont (1584-1616) and
John Fletcher (1579-1625): Help,
Medicine, Purgatory

Thomas Becon (1512-67): Wit

Sir Thomas Beecham (1879-1961):
Film Music

Henry Ward Beecher (1813-87):
Anger, Customs, Government,
Imagination, Law, Marriage,
Newspapers, Public Opinion, War

Thomas Beer (1889-1940): Poets

Sir Max Beerbohm (1872-1956):
Women

Aphra Behn (1640-89): Knowledge,
Money, Variety

Alan Bennett (1934-   ): Life

Arnold Bennett (1867-1931):
Husbands, Influenza, Journalists,
Justice, Undertakers

Jeremy Bentham (1748-1832):
Government

Tristan Bernard (1866-1947):
Sincerity

Ugo Betti (1892-1953): Nature

The Holy Bible (King James
Authorized Version): Anger,
Borrowers, Brawling Women,
Cheerfulness, Duty, Enemies,
Faith, Fame, Fear, Friends,
Giving, God, Good News, Great
Men, Hair, Happiness, Instruction,
Kings, Liberty, Love, Man,
Marriage, Mothers, Mothers-in-
Law, Opposition, Praise,
Rebellion, Sin, Speaking,
Stranger, Studies, Time, Training,
Vision, Wealth, Wisdom, Wives,
Women

Ambrose Bierce (1842-1914?):

Absentee, Accountability,
Acquaintances, Alliance,
Ambition, Bores, Chicago,
Clairvoyant, Conservative, Consul,
Consult, Contempt, Dictators,
Diplomacy, Egotist, Elector,
Emotion, Envelope, Ghost,
Happiness, History, Impartial,
Incompatibility, Interpreter,
Laughter, Lexicographer, Liberty,
Meekness, Novels, Patriot, Peace,
Politeness, Politics, Quorum,
Rebels, Women, Work

Caroline Bird (1915-   ): Career
Women

Otto von Bismarck (1815-98): Power

Sir William Blackstone (1723-80):
Kings

William Blake (1757-1827): Cunning,
Knowledge, Prison

Henry George Bohn (1796-1884):
Health

Nicolas Boileau (1636-1711): Fools

Henry St John, Viscount Bolingbroke
(1678-1751): Nations

Simon Bolivar (1783-1830): People's
Will

Daniel J. Boorstin (1914-   ):
Publicity

William Booth (1829-1912): England

Elizabeth Bowen (1899-1973): Fate

Mary Elizabeth Braddon (1837-
1915): Honeymoons

F.H. Bradley (1846-1924):
Metaphysics

Ann Bradstreet (1612-72): Love

Georges Braque (1882-1963): Truth

John Bright (1811-89): Force

Steuart Henderson Britt (1907-   ):
Advertising

Vera Brittain (1893-1970): Change,
Pacifists, Politics

Jacob Bronowski (1908-74): Studies

Anne Brontë (1820-49): But, Talents

Charlotte Brontë (1816-55):
Novelists, Prejudice

Index of Authors

G.K. Chesterton (1874-1936):
    Bigotry, Compromise,
    Government, Happiness, Novels,
    Puritans, Religion, Rich, Subjects
Agatha Christie (1890-1976): Habits,
    Murderers
Sir Winston Churchill (1874-1965):
    Americans, Appeaser, British,
    Capitalism, Change, Communism,
    Consultation, Credit, Criticism,
    Dictators, Diplomacy, End,
    Export, Failure, Free Speech,
    Frenchmen, Government,
    Headmasters, India,
    Irresponsibility, Prod,
    Quotations, Taunts, Victory, War
Cicero (106-43 BC): Law, Peace,
    Philosophers, Physicians,
    Politicians, Virtuous
William Cobbett (1762-1835):
    Independence
Sir Barnett Cocks (1907-   ):
    Committees
Frank Colby (1865-1925): Bottom,
    Humour
Hartley Coleridge (1796-1849):
    Freedom
Samuel Taylor Coleridge (1772-
    1834): Critics, Epigram,
    Freedom, Poets, Prayer, Singers
John Churton Collins (1848-1908):
    Advice, Faults
Mortimer Collins (1827-76): Age
George Colman (the Younger)
    (1762-1836): London
Rev. C.C. Colton (1780?-1832):
    Applause, Authorship, Books,
    Conversation, Corruption,
    Examinations, Genius, Happiness,
    Imitation, Knowledge, Law, Man,
    Ministers, Morality, Poets, Press,
    Professions, Religion, Rich, Ruin,
    Suicide, Talk, Truth, War, Writers
Confucius (551-479 BC): Beauty,
    Dislike, Learning, Modesty,
    Seeking, Studies, Success,

Women, Worry
William Congreve (1670-1729):
    Courtship, Husbands, Marriage,
    Music, Opinions, Women
Cyril Connolly (1903-74): Cities,
    Civilization, Happiness, Hell,
    Literature
Joseph Conrad (1857-1924):
    Ambition, Foes, Proverbs, Vanity
Calvin Coolidge (1872-1933):
    Prosperity, Strikes
James Fenimore Cooper (1789-
    1851): Democracy
Pierre Corneille (1606-84): Fear,
    Insults, Kings, Mercy, Over-
    Confidence, Victory
Hannah Cowley (1743-1809):
    Women
William Cowper (1731-1800):
    Frenchmen, God, Greenhouses,
    Grief, Nature, Talk, Wit

Roald Dahl (1916-   ): Nonsense
Nichiren Daishonin (1222-82):
    Abuse, Death, Itai Doshin, Life,
    Problems, Ruin, Treasure
Dante (1265-1321): Nature
Charles Darwin (1809-82):
    Shakespeare
Alphonse Daudet (1840-97): Love
Adelle Davis (1904-74): Health
Bette Davis (1908-   ): Discipline,
    Parents
Elmer Davis (1890-1958): Freedom
Charles de Gaulle (1890-1970): Great
    Men, Treaties
Thomas de Quincey (1785-1859):
    Memory
René Descartes (1596-1650): Mind
Destouches (Philippe Néricault)
    (1680-1754): Criticism
Charles Dickens (1812-70):
    Accidents, Poetry
Goldsworthy Lowes Dickinson
    (1862-1932): America
Benjamin Disraeli (1804-81):

174

Index of Authors

Education, Enemies, Error,
Example, Expectations, Faults,
Friends, Genius, Gentlemen, God,
Good Sense, Government, Habits,
Hate, Hope, Houses, Imitation,
Injuries, Innocence, Knowledge,
Law, Lawyers, Learning, Lending,
Life, Love, Marriage, Memory,
Mistresses, Moderation, Modesty,
Monarchy, Money, Neighbours,
Obedience, Pardon, Parley,
Passion, Patience, Peace,
Physicians, Playthings, Poverty,
Praise, Prosperity, Religion,
Rogues, Secrets, Success, Talk,
Talkers, Time, Travel, Vice,
Wealth, Well-bred, Wives, Words
Erich Fromm (1900-   ): Equality
Robert Frost (1874-1963): Home
J.A. Froude (1818-94): Experience,
Freedom
Thomas Fuller (1608-61): Happiness,
Music, Proverbs
Thomas Fuller (1654-1734):
Advantages, Advice, Anger,
Anglers, Blunders, Books,
Bravery, Chance, Clothes,
Command, Comparison,
Complaining, Conscience,
Cowards, Customs, Death,
Deception, Despair, Destiny,
Dexterity, Disappointment,
Distrust, Drunkenness, Enemies,
Envy, Excuses, Fame, Faults,
Fear, Flatterer, Fortune, Friends,
Gentlemen, Golden Age,
Gratitude, Great Minds, Habits,
Happiness, Hide, Hope,
Ingratitude, Innocence,
Innovations, Justice, Kindness,
Laughter, Law, Lawyers,
Learning, Lending, Liberty, Life,
Love, Marriage, May, Merit,
Money, Opportunities,
Overthrow, Passion, Pleasure,
Poets, Popular Opinion, Poverty,

Praise, Promises, Punishment,
Questions, Quiet, Religion,
Revenge, Rich, Ridicule, Self-
Preservation, Slander, Sleep, Slip
of the Tongue, Speaking,
Surprise, Talkers, Travel, Truth,
Wealth, Wisdom, Wives, Words

John Kenneth Galbraith (1908-   ):
Inflation, Progress
John Galsworthy (1867-1933):
Future, Justice
Mahatma Gandhi (1869-1948): Truth
Charles de Gaulle *see under* de Gaulle
John Gay (1685-1732): Life, Love,
Wives
David Lloyd George (1863-1945):
Poor
Henry George (1839-97): Progress
Edward Gibbon (1737-94): Advance,
Corruption, Education,
Independence, Revenge, Rich
W.S. Gilbert (1836-1911): Ancestry,
Life, Love, Policemen, Voting
Charlotte Perkins Gilman (1860-
1935): Plans
Jean Giraudoux (1882-1944):
Lawyers
William Gladstone (1809-98): Masses
Johann Wolfgang von Goethe (1749-
1832): Defects
Isaac Goldberg (1887-1938):
Diplomacy
Emma Goldman (1869-1940):
Anarchy, Government
Oliver Goldsmith (1728-74): Friends,
Law, Old, Silence, Wives, Women,
Writers
Baltasar Gracián (1601-58): Age,
Cheating, Fighting
Thomas Gray (1716-71): Glory

Lord Hailsham (1907-   ):
Arguments
J.B.S. Haldane (1892-1964): Science
Joseph Hall (Bishop of Norwich)

Index of Authors

Dean Inge (1860-1954): Democracy, Literature, Public Opinion

Robert G. Ingersoll (1833-99): Colleges, Meekness

Washington Irving (1783-1859): Age, Sharp Tongue

Mahalia Jackson (1911-72): Blues, Independence

Shirley Jackson (1920-65): February

Henry James (1843-1916): Historians, Novels, Observation

King James I of England and VI of Scotland (1566-1625): Tobacco

William James (1842-1910): Genius, Important, Indecision

Thomas Jefferson (1743-1826): Books, Delay, Liberty, Lying, Newspapers, Rebellion

Jerome K. Jerome (1859-1927): Love, Work

Douglas Jerrold (1803-57): Love, Religion

Sarah Orne Jewett (1849-1909): Tact

Samuel Johnson (1709-84): Amatorculist, Applause, Backfriend, Cark, Civilization, Conversation, Essay, Excise, Job, Knowledge, Language, Lexicographer, Life, London, Marriage, Oats, Patriotism, Patron, Pedants, Pension, Reading, Rich, Self-Confidence, Ships, Wife, Will, Words

Sir Keith Joseph (1918-): British

Joseph Joubert (1754-1824): Drums, Retraction

Juvenal (60?-140?): Badness

Immanuel Kant (1724-1804): Music

John Keats (1795-1821): Beauty, Failure, Imagination, Life, Love, Poetry, Sensations

Helen Keller (1880-1968): Life, Science

John F. Kennedy (1917-63): Communism, Conformity, Equality, Leadership, Negotiation, Peace, Revolution

Jean Kerr (1923-): Beauty

Ellen Key (1849-1926): Experience

John Maynard Keynes (1883-1946): Enterprise

Sören Kierkegaard (1813-55): Life

Henry King (1592-1669): Life, Silence

Martin Luther King (1929-68): Character, Church, Philanthropy

Rudyard Kipling (1865-1936): Cigars, England, Fun, Love, Women

Lisa Kirk (1925-): Conversationalists

Friedrich Gottlieb Klopstock (1724-1803): Poetry

Vicesimus Knox (1752-1821): Equality

Jean de La Bruyère (1645-96): Success, Women

Jean de La Fontaine (1621-95): Sadness

Duc de La Rochefoucauld (1613-80): Bores, Cleverness, Deception, Details, Eloquence, Fame, Friends, Happiness, Jealousy, Judgement, Justice, Love, Lovers, Man, Misfortunes, Money, People, Praise, Quarrels, Self-Confidence, Tranquillity

Alphonse de Lamartine (1790-1869): Life

Charles Lamb (1775-1834): Books, Human Species, Newspapers, Scotsmen

Elsa Lanchester (1902-): Comedians

Letitia Elizabeth Landon (1802-38): Poverty

Lao-tzu (c. 604-c. 531 BC): Boasting, Enlightenment, Trust

178

179

Index of Authors

Index of Authors

George Santayana (1863-1952):
America, Beauty, Fanaticism,
Habits
Jean-Paul Sartre (1905-80): War
Sir George Savile (1633-95):
Popularity
Dorothy L. Sayers (1893-1957):
Facts, Theories, Women
Friedrich von Schelling (1775-1854):
Architecture
Friedrich von Schiller (1759-1805):
Death
Friedrich von Schlegel (1772-1829):
Historians
Arthur Schopenhauer (1788-1860):
Fame, History, Marriage
C.P. Scott (1846-1932): Facts
Sir Walter Scott (1771-1832):
Deception, Life, Love
John Seldon (1584-1654): Kings,
Marriage
Seneca (c. 4 BC-65 AD): Art,
Behaviour, Crime, Drunkenness,
Genius, Man, Vice
Robert William Service (1874-1958):
Promises
Anna Sewell (1820-78): Knowledge
Thomas Shadwell (1642?-92): Sighs
William Shakespeare (1564-1616):
Bad News, Baldness, Beards,
Bible, Black Men, Borrowing,
Comfort, Cruelty, Death, Desire,
Drinking, Faces, Faith, Fathers,
Fear, Fierce, France, Friends,
Good, Greatness, Honesty, Hope,
Jealousy, Jews, Kisses, Laughter,
Lawyers, Life, Love, Lovers,
Lying, Marriage, Meals, Men,
Misery, Murder, Neglect,
Opinions, Parting, Past,
Peacemakers, Persuasion, Plots,
Praise, Pride, Remembrance,
Reputation, Rumour, Slander,
Smell, Talkers, Truth, Villains,
Winter, Wit, Women, World
George Bernard Shaw (1856-1950):
Actions, Artists, Assassination,
Cowardice, Democracy, Depair,
Duty, Efficiency, Englishmen,
Fear, Flattery, Gentlemen,
Golden Rule, Happiness, History,
Home, Liberty, Marriage, Money,
Parentage, Poverty, Professions,
Progress, Religion, Reminiscences,
Scoundrels, Teachers,
Temptation, Truth, Virtue
Percy Bysshe Shelley (1792-1822):
Hell, Poetry, Poets, Songs
William Shenstone (1714-63):
Commendation, Poets
Richard Brinsley Sheridan (1751-
1816): Conscience
Algernon Sidney (1622-83): Liars
Samuel Smiles (1812-1904):
Mistakes, Self-Help
Adam Smith (1723-90): Conspiracy,
Poverty
Alexander Smith (1830-67):
Happiness, Quotations
Horatio Smith (1779-1849):
Compliments
Logan Pearsall Smith (1865-1946):
Acquaintances, Aims, Authors,
Conscience, Fashionable, Liars,
Quarrels, Rich, Sorrow
Sydney Smith (1771-1845):
Laughter, Marriage
Tobias Smollett (1721-71):
Enjoyment, Prudence, Wisdom
Jan Christian Smuts (1870-1950):
Race Relations
Susan Sontag (1933-   ): Ambition
Sophocles (c. 495-406 BC): Advice,
Fate, Man, Success
Robert Southey (1774-1843): Life
Anna Garlin Spencer (1851-1931):
Preachers
Herbert Spencer (1820-1903):
Education, Health, Morality,
Opinions, Prejudice,
Republicanism, Science, Time
Benedict Spinoza (1632-77): Fame,

Index of Authors

Paul Valéry (1871-1945): Enemies,
 Politeness
Sir John Vanbrugh (1664-1726):
 Romance
Amy Vanderbilt (1908-74): Good
 Manners
Varro (116-27 BC): Wives
Luc de Clapiers, Marquis de
 Vauvenargues (1715-47):
 Achievement, Thoughts
Virgil (70-19 BC): Women
Voltaire (1694-1778): Beauty, Bores,
 Concerts, God, Government,
 History, Marriage, Prejudice,
 Work

Barbara Walters (1931-   ): Children
Artemus Ward (Charles Farrar
 Browne) (1834-67): Borrowing
Barbara Ward (1914-   ): Investment
Booker T. Washington (1856-1915):
 Dignity
George Washington (1732-99):
 Discipline, Peace
Auberon Waugh (1939-   ): British
 Employers
Evelyn Waugh (1903-66):
 Englishmen, News, Public
 Schools, Sexes, Welsh
Daniel Webster (1782-1852):
 Americans
H.G. Wells (1866-1946): England,
 History, Military, Moral
 Indignation, Nationality
Richard Whately (1787-1863):
 Happiness
Alfred North Whitehead (1861-
 1947): Civilization, Society
John Greenleaf Whittier (1807-92):
 Peace
George Whyte-Melville (1821-78):
 Commandments, Love
Ella Wheeler Wilcox (1855-1919):
 Laughter
Oscar Wilde (1854-1900): Art,
 Books, Charity, Conscience,
 Contradiction, Democracy,
 Diaries, Education, Examinations,
 Experience, Faithfulness, Faults,
 Generations, Genius, Gossip,
 Happiness, History, House of
 Lords, Hunting, Ideas, Ideals,
 Improbable, Information, Life,
 Literature, Love, Marriage,
 Parents, Peerage, People, Pleasure,
 Poetry, Poets, Poor, Reading,
 Relations, Religion, Repentance,
 Resolutions, Romance, Sin,
 Sincerity, Teachers, Temptation,
 Tory, Truth, War, Wickedness,
 Women
Thornton Wilder (1897-1975): Fools
Ludwig Wittgenstein (1889-1951):
 Clarity, Philosophy
P.G. Wodehouse (1881-1975): Aunts,
 Marriage
Virginia Woolf (1882-1941): Prose,
 Stately Homes
William Wordsworth (1770-1850):
 Poetry, Rainbow
Sir Henry Wotton (1568-1639):
 Ambassadors
Frank Lloyd Wright (1869-1959):
 Architects, Houses
William Wycherley (1640?-1716):
 Mistresses

W.B. Yeats (1865-1939): Comedy
Arthur Young (1741-1820): Angling,
 Property
Edward Young (1683-1765):
 Atheists, Procrastination

Israel Zangwill (1864-1926): America
Émile Zola (1840-1902): Truth

184